Brief Lives:
Charlotte Brontë

Jessica Cox

Brief Lives
Published by Hesperus Press Limited
4 Rickett Street, London sw6 1ru
www.hesperuspress.com

First published by Hesperus Press Limited, 2011

Designed and typeset by Fraser Muggeridge studio
Printed in Jordan by Jordan National Press

isbn: 978-1-84391-920-9

Contents

Introduction

'Literature cannot be the business of a woman's life:
and it ought not to be.'

This was the advice offered to the twenty-year-old Charlotte
Brontë in 1837 by the then Poet Laureate Robert Southey, to
whom she had written, with great deference, to ask his
opinion on a selection of her poetry. Within the letter, she expressed a desire '"to be forever known" as a poetess', prompting Southey's discouraging response. Replying to his letter,
the young Charlotte resolved to adhere to the advice given,
declaring earnestly, 'I trust I shall never more feel ambitious
to see my name in print; if the wish should rise, I'll look at
Southey's letter, and suppress it.' Despite her resolve, however,
she was ultimately to ignore Southey's advice, and to pursue
a career as a writer, producing one of the best-loved novels in
the English language, and leaving behind a legacy that even
her twenty-year-old self, who dreamed of literary success, can
scarcely have imagined.

The exchange between Southey and Brontë is illustrative
of a conflict that was to manifest itself in the author's writing
throughout her career, as she attempted to negotiate her position as both a woman and a writer at a time when strong preju-
dices against female authors prevailed: women, according to
traditional conventions, produced children; men produced great

literature. Southey's letter offered an early insight into the potential reception of her work. As a woman, Brontë would not have her literary productions judged on the same basis as those of her male counterparts – a fact of which she was all too aware, and which caused her considerable anxiety. The woman writer had risen to prominence with the increasing popularity of the novel from the late eighteenth century onwards. The novel was persistently viewed as inferior to poetry, though attitudes shifted somewhat as the nineteenth century progressed, with writers such as George Eliot, Henry James and, to a lesser extent, Brontë herself contributing to the establishment of the novel as a legitimate art form. Nevertheless, it continued to be perceived as an appropriate vehicle for the woman writer, and Southey's discouraging words are perhaps rooted in the notion that great poetry belonged strictly in the realm of the male writer. Brontë's anxieties on this front were ultimately to prove unfounded: she has long been celebrated as one of the greatest authors of the Victorian period, and, significantly, was one of very few women writers from the period to infiltrate the male-dominated canon prior to the explosion of interest in women's writing that accompanied the second-wave feminist movement of the 1960s and 1970s.

Charlotte Brontë's achievements are all the more significant given her relatively limited literary output. She published only a small selection of poems and three novels in her lifetime, with a fourth, *The Professor* (actually the first novel she wrote), published posthumously. Her letters, juvenilia and a fragment from an unfinished novel, *Emma*, also appeared in print after her death. Thus, while her name ranks alongside other Victorian literary greats such as Charles Dickens, William Makepeace Thackeray (to whom *Jane Eyre* is dedicated), George Eliot and Elizabeth Gaskell, her literary output does not. She died at the age of just thirty-eight, at a time when she was arguably displaying her greatest maturity as a writer. That her reputation should rest on such a small number of published works is extraordinary;

still more incredible is the fact that Brontë's fame (in the popular imagination at least) rests predominantly on a single novel: *Jane Eyre* a runaway success when it was first published in 1847, and never out of print since. Given her untimely death and limited output (she published less, even, than Jane Austen), her position as one of the literary giants of the Victorian period is truly remarkable.

If Brontë's fiction continues to fascinate, so too does her personal life. Charlotte Brontë's success story is extraordinary enough; that she should be one of three sisters to enjoy literary success is even more astonishing. The Brontë family were not wealthy; Patrick Brontë, Charlotte's father, was a clergyman living in Yorkshire. His wife, Maria Brontë, died when Charlotte was just five years old. The sisters may have been well-educated women by the standards of the time, but nevertheless their schooling was limited. The fascination with the Brontës' personal lives is undoubtedly partially rooted in the unlikelihood that one, let alone three literary geniuses should emerge from this rather obscure family, as well as in the tragedies that were to overtake them: Patrick Brontë lived to witness the deaths of all six of his children; Charlotte, at thirty-eight, was the longest lived. None of the six siblings left any known descendants (though there has been speculation that Branwell Brontë, Charlotte's brother, may have fathered an illegitimate child). Their story is truly tragic and their literary achievements appear to take on new meaning in light of their brief lives.

The purpose of this addition to the genre of Brontë biography is to provide a short introduction to Charlotte Brontë's life and work, and to consider some of the crucial issues relating to Brontë's development as a writer – in particular, her relationship with her sisters, her struggle to break the mould of the 'woman writer' and her negotiation of the public and private spheres. In constructing a brief account of her life, I return to her own writing as the basis for this work – her letters, diary fragments and fiction. Brontë's life, though somewhat short, was nevertheless rich: despite her relatively solitary life in Haworth (particularly after the death of her siblings), she corresponded with a large number of people, indicated by the fact that her collected letters total three substantial volumes. This book also seeks to examine the significance of the crucial relationship between what might be termed Brontë's public and private selves. In her early biography of Charlotte Brontë, published just two years after her subject's death, Elizabeth Gaskell highlights this divide between Brontë's public and personal lives, noting that 'Charlotte Brontë's existence [was] divided into two parallel currents – her life as Currer Bell, the author; her life as Charlotte Brontë, the woman. There were separate duties belonging to each character – not opposing each other; not impossible, but difficult to be reconciled.' As Gaskell implies, the relationship between these two selves was far from straightforward: through her fiction Brontë made public, in a sense, many of her private experiences, while at the same time concealing her private self behind the pseudonym Currer Bell. Following the deaths of her siblings, she struggled to overcome her private feelings of grief and loneliness in order to continue in her professional role as author. The revelation of her true identity forced a renegotiation of the relationship between her private and public selves as interest in her life and background increased. Throughout her literary career she combined her role as writer with that of dutiful daughter (though Elisabeth Jay suggests that this image of Charlotte is one constructed at Gaskell's discretion, noting that Brontë's first biographer chose 'to submerge Charlotte the writer in Charlotte the domestic saint').[1] Towards the end of her life, she took on the role of wife. Gender ideologies of the time dictated that there were separate spheres for men and women: men belonged to the public world of work; women to the private realm of home and hearth. Brontë demonstrated her awareness of this when she adopted her gender ambiguous pseudonym, and at times clearly struggled to negotiate her position within these two spheres.

The public fascination with the lives of the Brontës is largely responsible for the biographical tradition that has emerged and is partly fuelled by a desire to know the 'real' Charlotte Brontë the private, rather than the public figure. However, though we might distinguish between Brontë's 'public' writing, in the form of her published work, and her 'private' letters, both arguably entail a negation of the 'real' self: while the 'mask' of Currer Bell that Brontë adopted in order to publish her work is perhaps more evident than the mask she wears in her letters, there can be no question that she seeks to present an image that is not necessarily consistent with her true feelings in her letters as well as her fiction – as is arguably the case with all letters. Private diaries perhaps afford a clearer insight into a person's world than letters, but there are very few papers of this kind authored by Charlotte Brontë (a notable exception being the fragments that survive from her time at Roe Head school). While some of her letters are undoubtedly candid in their revelations of her feelings, thoughts and desires, there can be little doubt that they also conceal aspects of her life. Perhaps the strongest evidence of this is to be found in her letters to her lifelong friend, Ellen Nussey, whom she met at school at the age of fourteen. In a number of letters to Ellen, she expresses a desire that they might meet, in order to discuss issues that she would rather not allude to in a letter. Further, though the letters are indicative of a strong friendship between the two women, she concealed from Ellen her literary success, refusing to reveal herself as the author of *Jane Eyre*. Indeed, when rumour reached Ellen that Charlotte had authored a book, she was sternly rebuked by her friend, who vehemently denied that there was any truth in the rumour. The notion that Charlotte concealed aspects of herself from even those closest to her is further suggested in another letter written to Ellen in 1836, in which she declares, 'I am not like you. If you knew my thoughts, the dreams that absorb me, and the fiery imagination that at times eats me up, and makes me feel society, as it is, wretchedly insipid, you would pity and I dare say despise me.' The masks of

Charlotte Brontë are, therefore, multiple. She appears, through her letters, her fiction and others' accounts of her, as daughter, sister, friend, writer, and through these we are allowed glimpses into her world, but these various identities, though interlinked, are nevertheless disjointed, separate: we never quite see the complete woman. In this respect, the 'real' Charlotte Brontë remains elusive.

In spite of this, Charlotte Brontë and her family continue to fascinate, and the parallel interests in Brontë's personal life and her work are undoubtedly partly rooted in the discernible links between them. In the Hesperus Press title *Brief Lives: Jane Austen*, Fiona Stafford notes the disparity between Austen's life and fiction, stating that 'the gap between what is known of her life and what is apparent in her fiction is [...] clear.' In the case of Charlotte Brontë, however, her personal experiences undoubtedly manifest themselves in her fiction. It is inevitably problematic to place too much emphasis on the significance of authors' lives in relation to an understanding of their fictional works, to draw too many associations between writer and writing, to perceive a novel as a direct commentary on the life of the author, but, to some extent at least, Brontë must surely stand as an exception to this. Her life and fiction are replete with parallels: from the recurring figure of the absent mother in her novels, to the representation of her childhood experiences at Cowan Gate school in the Lowood scenes of *Jane Eyre*. The time she spent in Brussels, and in particular her relationship with and feelings for her teacher, M. Heger, provide source material for both *The Professor* and *Villette*, while her experiences as a teacher and governess assist in the portrayal of the protagonists' experiences in *Jane Eyre* and *Villette*. The Yorkshire landscape is a repeated source of inspiration in her writing, while her religious upbringing by her curate father and her liberal education clearly inform her work. Friends, acquaintances and local history and anecdotes also serve as significant sources of inspiration in her writing. It is difficult, therefore, to overestimate the extent to which her fiction is infused with her own personal experiences. Indeed, so close were some of the characters in *Shirley* to their real life counterparts that those who knew them were able to identify them as such.

If Brontë's fiction was influenced by her personal experiences, it was also influenced by her intense desire to succeed as a writer, and her awareness of the limitations placed on the woman writer. Throughout her career as an author, Brontë was perceptibly affected by reviewers' responses to her work: stung by criticism, and initially frustrated by the speculation as to her identity – particularly that relating to her sex. Such anxieties are referenced not only in her letters – her private writing – but in her published works as well. The first chapter of her novel *Shirley* can be seen as a direct response to criticism of *Jane Eyre* as overly dramatic and sensational, while it was only her publisher's refusal that prevented her from including a cutting response to Elizabeth Rigby's review of *Jane Eyre* in the Preface to *Shirley*. It is easy enough to believe that some of this anxiety at least is rooted in Southey's early response to her writing and her literary ambitions. One of my intentions, in this short biography, is to examine the extent to which such anxieties manifested themselves in Brontë's work, and influenced both her relationship with her sisters and her response to their work.

Brontë seems to have been constantly aware of the barriers that prevented her work from being judged on the same grounds as that of her male counterparts. In 1849, shortly after the publication of *Shirley*, she wrote to the critic G.H. Lewes on this subject, 'I wish you did not think me a woman: I wish all reviewers believed "Currer Bell" to be a man – they would be more just to him. You will – I know – keep measuring me by some standard of what you deem becoming to my sex – where I am not what you consider graceful – you will condemn me.' Although Charlotte was critical of her sister Anne's second novel, *The Tenant of Wildfell Hall*, she would, undoubtedly, have agreed with one of the assertions made in the Preface, 'If a book is a good one, it is so whatever the sex of the author may be.' She strove throughout her career to become not merely a successful *woman* writer, but a successful writer, whose accomplishments might be considered to rival those of her male contemporaries such as Dickens and Thackeray. In terms of the number of novels published, she is clearly their inferior; in terms of reputation, some 155 years after her death, her work remains as popular as ever.

Childhood

While Brontë's fiction is heavily influenced by her personal experiences, the portrayals of children in her novels appear to have little in common with her own childhood. The children in her fiction are often precocious or spoilt (Adèle and the Reed children in *Jane Eyre*; Polly in *Villette*), and appear to have more in common with those Charlotte was charged to teach during her two short stints working as a governess than with the Brontë children. Her fictional children are frequently isolated (Jane Eyre, Adèle), while Brontë was one of six children, and far from being spoilt with riches. She was born on 21st April 1816 in Thornton, near Bradford in Yorkshire, the third child of the Reverend Patrick Brontë and his wife, Maria. Their eldest child, also called Maria, was born two years earlier, followed by another daughter, Elizabeth, in 1815. Their only son, Patrick Branwell Brontë, was born the year after Charlotte, and followed by two more daughters – Emily, born in 1818, and Anne, born in 1820; hence just six years separated the six siblings.

Charlotte's father, Patrick, was of Irish descent. Born in 1777 in Drumballyroney in County Down, the eldest of ten children, at the age of sixteen he set up a school (a plan on which his daughters would also later embark), which he ran for a number of years before leaving Ireland in 1802 for England. There he became a student at St John's College, Cambridge, for the next four years. It would appear to be around this time that Patrick standardised the spelling of his surname to 'Brontë'. Records in Ireland suggest various spellings of the name – including 'Prunty' and 'Brunty' – and there has been much speculation over the shift to 'Brontë': perhaps a reference to the Cyclops in Greek mythology; possibly taken from Nelson's title, the Duke of Bronte. Some have suggested that the alteration was an attempt to obscure his relatively poor Irish background. Whatever the reasons may have been, the famous Brontë name as we now know it appears to have been introduced by Charlotte's father; with no known descendants, the family name was to disappear with Patrick's death (the British Surnames website, which uses information from the census, shows no one of that name in the United Kingdom today), though it lives on as one of the most famous literary names in history. Interestingly, the confusion over the name foreshadows his daughters' later attempts to conceal their own identities as authors by adopting the pseudonym 'Bell'.

After leaving Cambridge, Patrick entered the Church, and for the next few years held various curacies: first in Wethersfield in Essex, then Wellington in Shropshire, before moving, at the close of 1809, to Dewsbury in Yorkshire – the county with which his children would later become so closely associated. Patrick, like his children, harboured some literary aspirations, and in 1810, while living in Dewsbury, he published his first work, 'Winter Evening Thoughts: A Miscellaneous Poem'. Like his daughters, years later, Patrick appeared desirous to conceal his identity, and the work was published anonymously. Shortly after, he published a collection of poetry, entitled *Cottage Poems*. The poems, as one might expect from a curate, had a religious theme, and were intended, as he made clear in the Preface to the collection, for 'the lower classes of society'.[2] Over the course of his life, Patrick Brontë published a number of poems (including a second collection, entitled *The Rural Minstrel: A Miscellany of Descriptive Poems*, in 1813), stories (including a novella – *The Maid of Killarney* – in 1818), sermons, and pamphlets, as well as contributing articles and letters on current events to various periodicals and newspapers. Patrick did not achieve recognition as a writer, and indeed much of his writing was an extension of his work as a curate: didactic religious pieces intended to exert a wholesome influence on the reader. Nevertheless, he was to pass on his love of literature to his children. His publications formed part of their early reading, and his novella in particular was an important influence on their own early writings.[3]

From Dewsbury, Patrick moved a few miles away to the village of Hartshead in 1811. Like much of Yorkshire at this time, it was a manufacturing area, but when Patrick moved there, the industry was struggling because of the ongoing wars with France and the resulting economic climate. Tensions were high among workers and mill owners, and were exacerbated by the introduction of new machinery, which workers felt further threatened their livelihoods. Consequently, the years 1811 and 1812 saw a series of disturbances by disillusioned workers calling themselves 'Luddites', who carried out a number of attacks on manufacturers and their property. Patrick witnessed some of these disturbances first-hand during his curacy at Hartshead, and his memories – particularly of the attacks on Rawfolds Mill and its owner William Cartwright – were later fictionalised by his daughter Charlotte in her novel, *Shirley*.

It was in 1812, while curate of Hartshead, that Patrick met Maria Branwell, the woman he was to marry. Maria Branwell, Charlotte's mother, hailed from Penzance in Cornwall, where she was born in 1783. Like her husband, she came from a large family: she was the eighth of the eleven children of Thomas and Anne Branwell. Her father was a merchant, but died in 1808. Her mother died the following year, and when Patrick met Maria, she was staying with an aunt at Woodhouse Grove school near Bradford. Their marriage took place on 29th December 1812 at the church of St Oswald's in Guiseley, near Leeds. Marrying at the relatively late age of thirty-five, Patrick can hardly have expected to outlive his wife and all their children, but such was to be the case. Their first child, Maria, was born during Patrick's time as curate at Hartshead. Shortly after the birth of their second daughter, Elizabeth, the family moved to Thornton in Bradford. Following the birth of their youngest child, Anne, in 1820, Patrick removed his young family to the village of Haworth, where he took up the position of curate at St Michael and All Angels Parish Church. Charlotte Brontë was four years old when she moved to the parsonage in Haworth – the home where she was to spend the rest of her life.

Shortly after the family's removal to Haworth, Maria Brontë fell ill with what is now generally assumed to have been ovarian cancer. She died on 15th September 1821, at the age of thirty-eight (the same age as Charlotte at the time of her death thirty-four years later), leaving her husband a widower with six young children to support – the youngest of whom was just twenty months old. The impact of Maria Brontë's death on her children is evident in their writing: though the motherless heroine is a standard literary trope in nineteenth-century fiction, the writing of the three Brontë sisters is replete with absent mothers. Charlotte Brontë's most famous heroine, Jane Eyre, is an orphan; Jane's charge at Thornfield, Adèle, has also lost her mother; in *Shirley*, Caroline Helstone is brought up by her uncle after she is abandoned by her mother, while the eponymous heroine's mother is dead. William Crimsworth, the protagonist in *The Professor*, the first novel Charlotte wrote, is, like Jane Eyre, an orphan; while in her final novel, *Villette*, both Lucy Snowe and the young Polly are motherless. Mother figures are also notable for their absence in the work of Charlotte's sisters: Catherine Earnshaw's mother in Emily Brontë's *Wuthering Heights* dies when Catherine is seven, and Catherine herself dies shortly after the birth of her daughter. In Anne Brontë's *The Tenant of Wildfell Hall*, the heroine is raised by her aunt and uncle. It is only Anne's first novel, *Agnes Grey*, that stands apart from the rest of the Brontë novels in terms of the absent-mother theme. Most of the Brontë novels, with the notable exception of Charlotte Brontë's final completed novel, *Villette*, end with the marriage of the hero/heroine and with the birth of a new generation, or at least with the promise of children. Again, this is typical of nineteenth-century fiction, but given the authors' own maternal loss, such scenes take on a greater poignancy, seeming perhaps to further signify a yearning for the lost mother. Given Charlotte's young age at the time her mother died, her memories of her were undoubtedly few. In a poignant letter to Ellen Nussey, written almost thirty years after her mother's death, Charlotte, having been presented with a number of letters written by her mother to her father during their courtship, describes the experience of reading them:

I […] read them in a frame of mind I cannot describe – the papers were yellow with time all having been written before I was born – it was strange to peruse now for the first time the records of a mind whence my own sprang – and most strange – and at once sad and sweet to find that mind of a truly fine, pure and elevated order. They were written to papa before they were married – there is a rectitude, a refinement, a constancy, a modesty, a sense – a gentleness about them indescribable. I wished She had lived and that I had known her.

This desire to have known the lost mother infiltrates Charlotte's novels (as well as those of her sisters) – evident in her portrayals of motherless heroines whose quest for selfhood and identity can be seen to be linked in part to their motherless state.

Following the death of Maria Brontë, her sister, Elizabeth (after whom the second of the Brontë children was named), came to live at the parsonage in Haworth, initially on a temporary basis, but in fact remaining there until her own death in 1842. She was referred to by the children as Aunt Branwell, and her removal to Haworth was surely an attempt by Patrick Brontë to provide a maternal figure for his motherless children, something he was clearly concerned about. Following his wife's death, Patrick seems to have been determined to remarry and made a proposal of marriage, only three months after Maria Brontë's demise, to Elizabeth Firth, a friend of the family. He was refused, and subsequent attempts to find a wife also appear to have come to nought – no doubt at least partly because of the prospective wives' unwillingness to take on the burden of six young children. The law prevented Patrick from marrying his dead wife's sister, but her removal to Haworth meant she could at least offer some form of replacement for the lost mother. In a letter written shortly after his wife's death, Patrick referred to his sister-in-law as 'behaving as an affectionate mother to my children'. The arrangements at the parsonage after the death of Maria Brontë exerted a similar powerful influence on the later writings of the Brontë sisters. As with the lost mother, substitute maternal figures are a staple feature in the Brontës' fiction: aunts play a key role in the lives of both Jane Eyre and *The Tenant of Wildfell Hall*'s Helen Graham, while in *Villette* we are introduced to Lucy Snowe at her godmother's house.

Certainly in many respects Elizabeth Branwell sought to fill the place left by her sister, ensuring that her nieces acquired what she perceived as the necessary domestic skills. As well as supplying in part the maternal influence that the Brontë children lacked following the death of their mother, Aunt Branwell provided financial support to her nieces. She had an independent income of fifty pounds a year and was supportive of her nieces' endeavours to earn a living – offering one hundred pounds to help them set up a school in Haworth (a plan that never came to fruition). She was conservative in some respects, concerning herself with ensuring that the Brontë sisters were adept at those skills necessary for running a household. Although their own household employed various servants, including Tabitha Ackroyd, who worked for the family for thirty years, and to whom the Brontë children were devoted, the young Brontë sisters nevertheless assisted with domestic duties throughout their lives, often combining their avid interest in books with such work: in her biography of Brontë, Gaskell includes an anecdote describing Emily baking bread in the kitchen while learning German from a book opened in front of her. Indeed, Gaskell claims that the Brontë sisters were taught 'by their aunt [...] that to take an active part in all household work was, in their position, woman's simple duty'. Hence, Charlotte, Emily and Anne were encouraged to fulfil the duties traditionally prescribed to women of their class. Nevertheless, Aunt Branwell was liberal enough to support her nieces' ambitions to earn an independent living. Charlotte, Emily and Anne inherited several hundred pounds from their aunt after her death, which was used to help finance the publication of their poems, as well as *Wuthering Heights* and *Agnes Grey*.

Aunt Branwell could be difficult at times – objecting to visitors, for example – and occasionally ill-tempered, but it is clear that she cared deeply for her sister's children, and that they in turn loved and respected her. Certainly there is little evidence to support the image of Elizabeth Branwell as a tyrannical figure in the Brontë household, as some biographers and scholars have suggested.[4] Branwell in particular was close to his aunt: writing to a friend during her final illness, he declared that she 'has been for twenty years as my mother'. After her death he wrote, 'I have now lost the [guide] and director of all the happy days connected with my childhood.'

Despite the assistance of his sister-in-law, Patrick Brontë must have struggled to raise his six children. Elizabeth Gaskell paints Patrick as something of a tyrannical father to his young children (thus further contributing to the various myths surrounding the Brontë family). She suggests that 'he was not naturally fond of children, and felt their frequent appearance on the scene as a drag both on his wife's strength and as an interruption to the comfort of the household.' In the first edition of her biography, she includes an account from a woman who had nursed Charlotte's mother in her final illness, stating that Patrick Brontë 'thought that children should be brought up simply and hardily: so they had nothing but potatoes for their dinner', though, at Patrick Brontë's request, she deleted this passage from subsequent editions, along with an account of Patrick Brontë's destroying a pair of boots because he believed them to be 'too gay and luxurious for his children'. Anecdotes of Charlotte's father eating alone in his study, firing his gun from the back door and apparently mindlessly destroying household property when angered reinforce the image of the neglectful, tyrannical father figure. However, there is much to suggest that this was far from being the case. Some of the earliest surviving letters from Charlotte to her father are affectionate and playful and she remained a devoted daughter for the rest of her life. In a letter to her brother, Branwell, she refers to 'our dear papa', and there is nothing to indicate that she wished to escape her father's presence – indeed, to the contrary, she rejected several proposals of marriage that would have enabled her to leave the parsonage and her father had she chosen.

Evidence from Patrick himself suggests he was keenly concerned with and involved in his children's development and education. One particular recollection, detailed in Gaskell's biography, provides a fascinating insight not only into Patrick's relationship with his children, but into the minds of the young Brontë children as well. In an attempt to encourage his children to overcome their timidity and speak their minds, Patrick provided them with a mask. Instructing them to 'speak boldly from under cover of the mask', he asked them each questions in turn, and describes Charlotte's responses. She was then around eight years old: 'I [...] asked Charlotte what was the best book in the world; she answered, "The Bible". And what was the next best; she answered, "The Book of Nature".' In response to the questions put to his other children, he learned that Anne desired 'Age and experience'; Emily advised her father to reason with her naughty brother, and failing that to whip him; Branwell felt that the difference in the intellects of men and women could be ascertained 'by considering the difference between them as to their bodies'; Elizabeth believed the 'best mode of education for a woman was "That which would make her rule her house well"'; and Maria believed her time was best spent in preparing for 'a happy eternity'. Taken together, the children's answers suggest a religious devotion and an acceptance of conventional gender roles, yet the older Charlotte was, at various points in her life, to question both these assumptions. While the anecdote is indicative of the interest Patrick took in his children, the mask behind which the Brontë children hid themselves while answering their father's questions anticipates the mask behind which Charlotte, Emily and Anne would later conceal their true identities and their gender – writing and publishing as Currer, Ellis and Acton Bell respectively. Like her younger self, the older Charlotte Brontë was to 'speak boldly from under cover of the mask', concealing her true identity and her gender behind the name of Currer Bell.

When Charlotte was eight years old, she left Haworth for the first time since her arrival four years previously. Anxious that his daughters should be able to make their own way in the world, in 1824, Patrick Brontë sent his four eldest daughters to the Cowan Bridge Clergy Daughters' school – some forty miles from Haworth – to continue their education. Charlotte arrived in August, and, though she was only to remain there for a matter of a few months, the experience was to haunt her for the rest of her life, finding its way into her fiction in the form of the Lowood scenes in *Jane Eyre*. The school was founded by the Reverend William Carus Wilson, the original for Mr Brocklehurst in *Jane Eyre*, and its stated aim was the pupils' 'intellectual and religious improvement', which would enable them 'to maintain themselves in the different stations of life to which Providence may call them'.[5] As well as receiving instruction in various subjects, pupils were also expected to perform those duties associated with domestic servants, in preparation for future employment. A broader educational programme was available at an extra charge for those pupils likely to embark on careers as governesses or teachers, and Charlotte, along with Maria and Emily, was enrolled on this basis: a clear indication of the path Patrick foresaw his daughters following. The admissions register detailing Charlotte's abilities on her arrival at the school informs us that she 'reads tolerably – Writes indifferently – Ciphers a little and works neatly. Knows nothing of Grammar, Geography, History or Accomplishments'[6] – a rather critical assessment, and certainly not indicative of her later achievements.

The regime at the school was strict, and conditions harsh. A few months after the arrival of Charlotte and her sisters, Maria Brontë fell ill. In spite of the fact that she was clearly suffering, she was nevertheless forced to attend her lessons, and her family at Haworth remained unaware of her declining health for some time. Eventually, in February 1825, Patrick Brontë was contacted by the school and informed of his eldest daughter's illness. He travelled to Cowan Bridge and removed Maria from the school: it was the last time Charlotte would see her eldest sibling. Maria was suffering from pulmonary tuberculosis (then commonly known as consumption). Following her departure from Cowan Bridge, she survived for several weeks, but eventually succumbed to the illness and died on 6th May 1825, at the age of just eleven. Just over three weeks later, Elizabeth Brontë was also returned home to the parsonage; like her elder sister, she was suffering from consumption. The return from the school of a second seriously ill daughter led Patrick to remove his remaining children from Cowan Bridge, and Charlotte and Emily arrived home on 1st June. Elizabeth died just two weeks after her removal from Cowan Bridge, on 15th June. Within the space of a little over a month, Patrick Brontë had buried his two eldest children, who were laid to rest next to their dead mother. The family of six children was now reduced to four, and Charlotte found herself suddenly in the position of the eldest child of the family, and, whether expected to or not, took on her shoulders some of the responsibility that she perceived this to entail – a role previously fulfilled by her eldest sister, Maria: giving an account of the children to Elizabeth Gaskell, one of the Brontës' servants recalled that Maria 'was as good as a mother to her sisters and brother'. Following the death of the two eldest Brontë children, this responsibility now fell to Charlotte.

As with the death of her mother, the profound impact of the deaths of her two elder sisters is reflected in Charlotte's fiction. Jane's experiences at Lowood school in *Jane Eyre* are clearly based on the short time Charlotte spent at Cowan Bridge, and early readers of the novel were able to identify the original of Lowood as Cowan Bridge from her descriptions. Charlotte, rightly or wrongly, blamed Carus Wilson and the conditions at the school for the deaths of her sisters and her bitterness is suggested by her portrayal of Lowood. Certainly, conditions at Cowan Bridge were harsh and the school appears to have failed to recognise the severity of Maria and Elizabeth's conditions. However, tuberculosis was common throughout the nineteenth century and would later claim the lives of Charlotte's remaining siblings. Conditions at the school may have contributed in as far as the proximity of a large number of pupils meant that infectious diseases were likely to spread, while a poor diet and generally unsanitary conditions may have served to weaken immune systems, but the extent to which Carus Wilson can be held directly responsible is questionable. Gaskell seems to have sympathised with Charlotte's understandable bitterness towards the school, and was extremely critical of the conditions at Cowan Bridge in her biography. The association of Brocklehurst in *Jane Eyre* and Carus Wilson has further increased the popular notion of the founder of the school as culpable in the deaths of the two eldest Brontë children, though Carus Wilson himself strongly refuted a number of the accusations levelled at him: Gaskell was threatened with legal action over her comments about Cowan Bridge and its founder, and consequently tempered at least some of her accusations in the third edition of her biography.

Charlotte's grief at the deaths of her two sisters provided the source material for the death of Helen Burns in *Jane Eyre*, who is based specifically on Charlotte's eldest sister, Maria Brontë. For Charlotte, Maria represented something of a maternal influence, as Helen does for Jane, the loss being all the more painful for Charlotte in light of the death of her mother. Charlotte's letters contain few references to her two elder sisters, but it is clear from Gaskell's recollections of conversations with Charlotte, as well as from Charlotte's own letters to her publishers, that she drew on the experience of her sister's death in portraying the death of Helen Burns. The scene is full of pathos not only because of the glimpse it affords of the grief Charlotte experienced as a child on the death of her sisters, but also because it unwittingly seems to anticipate Anne Brontë's death just a short time later:

> I am very happy, Jane; and when you hear that I am dead, you must be sure and not grieve: there is nothing to grieve about. We all must die one day, and the illness which is removing me is not painful; it is gentle and gradual: my mind is at rest [...] by dying young, I shall escape great sufferings [...] I am going to God [...] I can resign my immortal part to him without any misgiving[.]

Anne, like Helen Burns, was to die resigned to her fate and with complete faith in God. Writing of her youngest sister's death to her publisher, William Smith Williams, Charlotte revealed how Anne 'died without struggle – resigned – trusting in God – thankful for release from a suffering life – deeply assured that a better existence lay before her'.

Early Writing

Following the deaths of their two elder sisters, Charlotte and Emily were, unsurprisingly, permanently removed from the school at Cowan Bridge and, for the next few years, educated at home, with Patrick Brontë taking on much of the burden of educating his children himself, despite the demands on his time. The books belonging to the Brontë household during Charlotte's childhood suggest her education at the parsonage included history, grammar, geography and literature, as well as an emphasis on religious and moral education. In addition to this, despite his limited income (barely sufficient to support his large family), Patrick also hired an art tutor and a music tutor for his children, in an attempt to ensure that Charlotte and her siblings were provided with every opportunity for their creative and intellectual development.

The formative education of the Brontë children was clearly crucial to their later development as writers. However, the structured education Charlotte received during her short time at Cowan Bridge and the formal lessons with her tutors were undoubtedly less important in terms of this development than the informal, liberal education she received at the parsonage. All of the Brontë children were avid readers, and their father refused to censor their reading; hence from a young age they were allowed access to works that might generally be perceived as unsuitable for young minds – particularly for the daughters of the family, at a time when women's reading material was frequently heavily censored. The Brontë children eagerly consumed newspapers, magazines, and whatever books they could lay their hands on, and these exerted a powerful influence on their creative development. When Elizabeth Gaskell came to write her biography of Charlotte, Patrick provided some information relating to his children's early development as writers:

When mere children, as soon as they could read and write, Charlotte and her brother and sisters, used to invent and act little plays of their own [...] I discovered signs of rising talent, which I had seldom or never before seen, in any of their age.

In 1826, Patrick Brontë made a gift to his only son of a box of toy soldiers – a seemingly trivial event that was, in fact, to prove central to the artistic development of the Brontë children. The twelve-year-old Charlotte provides an account of the gift and its consequences in a diary paper entitled 'The History of the Year', dated 12th March 1829. It details the crucial development in the imaginative worlds of the four remaining Brontë children:

Papa bought Branwell some soldiers at Leeds. When Papa came home it was night we were in bed so next morning Branwell came to our door with a box of soldiers. Emily and I jumped out of bed and I snatched up one and exclaimed this is the Duke of Wellington it shall be mine!! When I said this Emily likewise took one and said it should be hers. When Anne came down she took one also. Mine was the prettiest of the whole and perfect in every part. Emily's was a grave looking fellow [and] we called him Gravey. Anne's was a queer little thing very much like herself. He was called Waiting Boy. Branwell chose Bonaparte[.]

The gift of the soldiers led to some of the children's earliest writings, for example the stories of the Young Men, recorded in minute, barely legible writing in tiny books, a number of which survive today. Charlotte's childish description of this event provides some interesting insights into the relationship between the siblings, as well as into her development as a writer. The soldiers are presented to Branwell, the only boy, and of the three remaining sisters, it is Charlotte, now the eldest, who makes her selection first, followed by Emily, and lastly Anne – suggesting a distinct 'pecking order' in the family based on sex and age. Though this is merely a child's account of a father's gift, it does seem telling in terms of the future relationship between the siblings: Charlotte was shortly to form a creative alliance with Branwell, Emily with Anne. Though the sisters would later collaborate on their volume of poetry, and frequently discuss their work with one another, offering each other advice and support, it would seem naive to suppose that there existed no sibling rivalry between them – a rivalry that almost certainly came into play later in their lives as they attempted to publish their first novels, and which arguably continued to affect Charlotte even after her sisters' deaths.

Charlotte's alliance with her brother was perhaps, even at this young age, in part a strategic move: the eldest surviving child, Charlotte, allied with the only son, Branwell, for whom the family had high hopes of success. In a letter written many years later, shortly after her brother's death, she revealed that her father 'naturally thought more of his only son than of his daughters'. Implicit in this is an awareness that her gender would not only affect her potential reception as a writer, but that it also had a profound effect on her personal life: as a daughter, even in her new position as the eldest child of the family, she could not expect to obtain the same high opinion from her father that he bestowed on his son. Evidence suggests that during her childhood Charlotte felt closer to her brother than to either of her surviving sisters, perhaps because they were closer in age, or perhaps because she recognised in her brother a similar sense of ambition to her own. In a letter to him written in 1832, she writes, 'As usual I address my weekly letter to you – because to you I find the most to say.' Though various circumstances may have contributed to Charlotte's early partnership with her brother, it would seem to anticipate her later desire to be considered alongside the male writers of the day: perhaps even at this young age, she recognised that the male sex was granted far more privileges and opportunities than women.

The literary alliance between Charlotte and Branwell was to continue for several years. Together they created the 'Young Men's Magazine' and 'Branwell's Blackwoods Magazine' (the title of the latter taken from their favourite publication of the day), in which they recorded the stories of the Young Men. Over the years that followed, Charlotte wrote almost incessantly: Margaret Smith, editor of Brontë's letters, estimates that she wrote around 180 poems and 120 stories between 1829 and 1841, though, as an unknown number of her early literary productions have not survived, this may well be a conservative estimate. Many of these works were based around an imaginary colony in Africa, which the Brontë children named Glass Town. The Glass Town stories eventually led to the creation of two new imaginary worlds: Angria, created by Charlotte and Branwell, and Gondal, the creation of Emily and Anne. Again, Charlotte's alliance with Branwell, rather than her two sisters, can be perceived as significant, and the creation of Angria and Gondal seems to indicate a distinct divide between the two sets of siblings. Emily and Anne's Gondal saga has not survived, other than in passing references in diary papers and in some of Emily's poetry, which has its roots in her Gondal writings, but from which she later removed references to this imaginary world. However, much of the Angrian writing of Charlotte and Branwell has survived.

Though Charlotte's early fictional writings inevitably suggest the immaturity of the author, they are nevertheless significant in terms of their relationship to and anticipation of her later literary productions, as well as a useful indication of her key literary influences at this age. If the Angrian writings lack the maturity of Charlotte's later novels, they are notable for their reflection of a youthful literary mind unrestrained by the conditions of the Victorian literary marketplace. Charlotte Brontë's early literary productions have more in common with Romantic writing than Victorian realism. There is an emphasis on the gothic and the sensational, which she would later attempt to eschew, not entirely successfully, in favour of literary realism. The exotic locations, Byronic heroes and high passions of the juvenilia anticipate *Jane Eyre* to some extent, but these features are far more pronounced here. Adultery, illegitimacy and sexual desire are all unflinchingly portrayed: the young Charlotte, writing for pleasure rather than publication, had no need to concern herself with notions of public propriety. Such themes found their way into her novels later in life, but in diluted form – rendered more palatable for public taste, though even then she would be accused of 'coarseness'. She would later criticise her sister Anne for writing a novel in which the heroine suffers various indignities through her marriage to her dissolute husband, but in her juvenilia she has no such qualms. In this respect, her early writing is suggestive of the mask she would later adopt as 'Currer Bell': not only concealing her true identity but arguably repressing certain tendencies in her writing as well – whether this was the result of a desire for literary success and public acknowledgment, or whether it marks a genuine shift in her writing style is debatable (though the first novel she wrote, *The Professor*, perhaps suggests the latter).

If the juvenilia are important for their thematic anticipation of the later novels, and in their reflection of a writer free from constraints, they are also significant in terms of gender – as we have seen, a key issue in Brontë's novels, as well as in her choice of pseudonym. While Anne and Emily place a female character – Augusta Geraldine Almeda – at centre stage, it is the figure of the Byronic (anti)hero that dominates Charlotte's Angrian world. This figure begins life as the Duke of Wellington – the identity selected for Charlotte's toy soldier – and subsequently takes on the identity of the Duke of Wellington's son, Arthur Wellesley, who goes on to become Marquis of Douro, the Duke of Zamorna, and finally King of Angria. Elsewhere in the juvenilia, it is Charles Wellesley, brother of Arthur, who narrates the story. The emphasis on the figure of the hero, rather than the heroine, anticipates Charlotte Brontë's first novel, *The Professor*, with its first-person male narrator, William Crimsworth, and of course Charlotte's later adoption of a gender-ambiguous pseudonym, although she would later deviate from the pattern apparent in her early writing through her emphasis on specifically female experience in her portrayals of her heroines – Jane Eyre, Shirley Keeldar, Caroline Helstone and Lucy Snowe. Her early interest in the figure of the hero can perhaps be attributed in part to the influence of Branwell.

The imaginary worlds of Glass Town and Angria were to dominate Charlotte's formative years as a writer, and, along with her siblings, she became entirely absorbed in the fictional world she had created, to the extent that the boundaries between reality and imagination appear blurred at times. The diary papers that survive detail everyday life at the parsonage alongside events occurring in the imaginary worlds of their creation, and, particularly during the times she spent away from Haworth, the world of Angria provided a key source of comfort and consolation for Charlotte, enabling her to escape the harsh realities of her everyday life, and return to the world of her imagination in which she found so much solace and comfort. This blurring of the boundaries is further apparent in the fiction itself, in which the children flit in and out as narrators and sometimes participants in the stories. From a young age, then, though external circumstances may have forced her to take a different path, Charlotte was immersed in the world of her imagination.

In January 1831, at the age of fourteen, Charlotte again left the parsonage to continue her formal education – this time at

Roe Head school in Mirfield (twenty miles from Haworth). The school was run by Margaret Wooler (the original for Miss Temple in *Jane Eyre*) and her four sisters, and Charlotte's time here was in stark contrast to the miserable few months she had spent at Cowan Gate. Amongst those people she met at Roe Head were fellow pupils Ellen Nussey and Mary Taylor, both of whom would become lifelong friends (of whom Charlotte had relatively few outside of her immediate family) and regular correspondents (indeed, Charlotte's letters to Ellen and Mary form the basis of much of what we know about her life and views). Assisting Elizabeth Gaskell with her research for her biography years later, Mary Taylor recalled the first impression Charlotte made on her upon her arrival at Roe Head: 'I first saw her coming out of a covered cart, in very old-fashioned clothes […] She looked a little old woman, so short-sighted that she always appeared to be seeking something […] She was very shy and nervous, and spoke with a strong Irish accent.' Despite having spent her entire life in Yorkshire, it seems Charlotte's accent betrayed her father's Irish roots.

Though her experiences at Roe Head were largely positive, Charlotte was afflicted by the homesickness that was subsequently to affect her whenever she left her family and home in Haworth. She no doubt lacked a sense of belonging upon her arrival at the school, and her sense of dislocation at being removed from her family rendered her experience at Roe Head somewhat painful at first. She delighted, however, in the formation of her friendships with Mary Taylor and Ellen Nussey; indeed, her letters from this period suggest an element of surprise that they should take a continuing interest in her – indicative, perhaps, of her own impression of herself as something of an outsider. Though she was widely read, her education had been somewhat sporadic, and this gave her fellow pupils the impression of ignorance. Despite Patrick's efforts to educate his children, upon Charlotte's arrival at Roe Head, her limited knowledge in matters such as geography and grammar was noted by her fellow pupils. Nevertheless, she went on to excel as a pupil there, and was awarded the school prize for achievement three times during the short period she spent at the school.

In June 1832, Charlotte left Roe Head and returned to Haworth, where she made use of the formal education she had received over the last eighteen months by assisting in her sisters' learning. She remained in touch with both Mary Taylor and Ellen Nussey, and a few months after her departure from Roe Head, visited Ellen at her family home in Birstall, West Yorkshire, for the first time. This was followed by a visit from Ellen to Haworth the following year, and Charlotte's letters from this period attest to a deepening friendship between the two. Though Charlotte had extended her field of friends and acquaintances, her intense attachment to her siblings, and to Branwell in particular, continued. Following her return to Haworth, she once again turned to the imaginary worlds she had inhabited since childhood.

In July 1835, Charlotte returned to Roe Head school – this time as a teacher (anticipating Jane's progression from pupil to teacher at Lowood in *Jane Eyre* and further highlighting the autobiographical links between heroine and author). Charlotte was nineteen when she took up her post as teacher, and found her first position difficult at times. Once again, she was severely affected by the removal from home and family: shortly before she left to take up her post, she wrote to Ellen, informing her that, 'We are all about to divide, break up, separate.' She was somewhat comforted, however, by the presence of Emily, who accompanied her sister to Roe Head as a pupil, though the younger sister was to suffer even more acutely from a sense of overwhelming homesickness. Indeed, such was Emily's anguish at her removal from Haworth and her beloved moors that she only remained at Roe Head a few months, and was replaced by Anne in October of that year. Charlotte was to remain as a teacher at Miss Wooler's school until December 1838. During this time, she continued to nurse literary ambitions, and felt acutely the contrast between these hopes and dreams and her life as a teacher. This conflict is revealed in a number of personal papers from this period. The papers stand in stark contrast to Charlotte's letters, and are indicative of the fact that, even with those she felt closest to, she tended to conceal her true feelings in her correspondence. Few such papers survive (indeed, it is unclear whether or not Charlotte regularly recorded her feelings in this way): those that do are crucial in providing further evidence of the various masks that Charlotte Brontë adopted, and allow us a brief and tantalising glimpse of the woman behind the masks.

Though separated from her brother, in her free moments Charlotte continued to focus on their imaginary world of Angria, and it was a subject of discussion between the two in their correspondence. Writing one of the diary papers shortly after receiving a letter from Branwell, in which he included an imagined letter from Northangerland to his daughter, she states, 'I lived on its contents for days' – again indicating the significance of their early creative projects to her later development as a writer, but also suggesting the extent to which she obsessed over her imaginary world, which provided a crucial source of escapism during her time at Roe Head. These fragmentary diary papers drift between the world of Roe Head and that of Angria, as Charlotte's musings on her imaginary world are frequently interrupted by the realities of life as a teacher. She had little time to focus on the Angrian world of her imagination, and felt her teaching duties to be a frustrating burden at times, giving vent to her feelings in another of the diary papers from this period:

The thought came over me am I to spend all the best part of my life in this wretched bondage, forcibly suppressing my rage at the idleness the apathy and the hyperbolical & most asinine stupidity of these fat headed oafs and on compulsion assuming an air of kindness, patience & assiduity?

The six fragmentary papers that survive from this time speak of the excessive emotion of the writer, forced to repress her rage and frustration and adopt the mask of willing teacher. Referring to a particularly frustrating encounter with a pupil, she writes, 'She nearly killed me between the violence of the irritation her horrid wilfulness excited and the labour it took to subdue it to a moderate appearance of calmness.' It is hardly surprising that Charlotte does not reveal her true emotions in her letters from this period, at a time when excessive emotion, in women in particular, was frequently linked to notions of madness. The contrast between the image of Charlotte the respectable teacher and Charlotte the deeply frustrated, sometimes enraged writer seems to anticipate much later critical readings of *Jane Eyre*, which posit the character of the madwoman, Bertha Mason, as a representation of Jane's 'secret self', succumbing to the passion and rage that Jane herself must learn to suppress in order to survive.

In the moments she spent alone at Roe Head, Charlotte was sometimes overwhelmed by the desire to write, but was seemingly inevitably interrupted by one of her pupils, whom she scathingly refers to in her diary papers as 'dolts' and 'asses': her duties as a teacher seemed irreconcilable with her desire to become a writer, and she was almost tortured by 'a feeling that I cannot satisfy', a desire to escape the mundane drudgery of her life, and to return to the inspiring moors of Haworth where she might pursue her literary ambitions. She had, up until this point in her life, experienced an unusual degree of freedom – largely the result of her liberal home education, which enabled her and her siblings both the creative freedom to write and invent stories and plays, and the physical freedom to roam the moors behind the parsonage. On arriving to take up her position as teacher at Roe Head, she found this freedom suddenly and brutally curtailed by the demands that were now placed upon her. Teaching failed to provide the intellectual stimulation to which she had become accustomed, yet she was compelled to try and earn a living. In this respect, her situation mirrored that of numerous nineteenth-century women (though Charlotte was perhaps better educated and more intellectually inclined than many), for whom opportunities were few, and who frequently had little choice but to take up a career as governess or teacher. Charlotte's response to the intellectual stagnation that threatened to overwhelm her was to retreat further into the world of her imagination, as the Roe Head journals testify.

Charlotte's time at Roe Head proved tumultuous not only because she was struggling to reconcile her occupation as a teacher with her literary ambitions, but also because she suffered increasingly from a crisis of identity linked to her religious beliefs, which fed in to her increasing sense of isolation and depression. With her father an Anglican clergyman, Charlotte had been raised a devout Christian, and her faith in God appears to have remained constant throughout her life. However, she struggled with the doctrines of the Church, and appears, at various points in her life, to have considered the implications of both Calvinist and Catholic doctrine: the former, in particular, caused her considerable anxiety at this time. Attempting to articulate her sense of religious melancholy, she wrote to Ellen, 'I know the treasures of the Bible I love and adore them. I can see the Well of Life in all its clearness and brightness; but when I stoop down to drink of the pure waters they fly from my lips as if I were Tantalus.' It is unclear what provoked this apparent religious crisis, but it was linked (whether as cause or effect) to an increasing sense of self-loathing. She dwelt extensively on the doctrines of predestination prescribed by Calvinism, and convinced herself that, 'If Christian perfection be necessary to Salvation I shall never be saved.' Significantly, Anne too suffered from a religious crisis during her time at Roe Head, and, as with Charlotte, appears to have reflected painfully on the possible implications of Calvinist doctrine. It seems clear with hindsight that Charlotte suffered from extensive bouts of depression throughout her life. These were often linked to external events, such as the deaths of her sisters, but her increasing sense of isolation and the inner conflict between teacher and would-be writer clearly prompted the sense of despair that appears to have enveloped her during her time at Roe Head.

Employment

Charlotte's source of comfort while she struggled with her religious beliefs and sense of identity at Roe Head was her imagination. Both Charlotte and Branwell continued to harbour literary ambitions and in 1837 they wrote to two of the greatest poets of the day with samples of their poetry: Branwell to William Wordsworth and Charlotte to Robert Southey, in response to which she received his discouraging reply and appears, for a time at least, to have resolved to abandon her poetic ambitions. However, while she may have resolved not to seek fame and fortune as a poet, she continued to write, producing a large number of poems during her time at Roe Head.

Towards the close of 1837, an incident occurred at the school that must have recalled to Charlotte's mind her time at Cowan Bridge and her elder sisters' illnesses and subsequent deaths. Since that period, Charlotte had experienced a feeling of dread whenever anyone of her acquaintance suffered from those symptoms that might be associated with consumption (a dread that was to afflict her for the rest of her life). She must, therefore, have been overtaken by a sense of panic when her sister, Anne, fell ill, losing her voice and apparently experiencing trouble breathing. Inevitably, Charlotte recalled the final illnesses of her two elder sisters, and was therefore deeply distressed when Miss Wooler appeared to dismiss Anne's symptoms as nothing of concern. The event led to a dispute between Charlotte and her employer, and the two sisters returned to Haworth, where Anne recovered. Though she had severely reprimanded Miss Wooler for her attitude towards her sister's illness, and resolved not to return to Roe Head, the two were reconciled somewhat before Charlotte's departure, and in January 1838, she agreed to return to her position as teacher.

Charlotte remained an employee of Roe Head school for much of the year that followed, but she continued to suffer with extensive bouts of depression, accompanied by hypochondria – possibly exacerbated by the fact that Anne, following her bout of illness, had not returned to Miss Wooler's school, and Ellen, who lived within visiting distance of the school, was then away from home; hence Charlotte must have felt even more isolated. She refers in a letter to Ellen to the 'weeks of mental and bodily anguish' she suffered, and eventually, following medical advice, she returned to Haworth in order to try and recover her spirits. The time she spent at the parsonage in Haworth appears to have had the desired effect, and she subsequently returned to Miss Wooler's school, which had now moved to Dewsbury Moor, a few miles from its original location. Eventually, however, Charlotte felt that she could no longer endure her life as a teacher, and, before departing for Haworth for the Christmas vacation in 1838, she informed Miss Wooler that she would not be returning.

Though she was deeply unhappy for much of her time at Roe Head, her experiences there exerted a powerful influence on her later fiction. Governesses and teachers feature in all of Charlotte's novels – a motif for which she drew on her own personal experiences. As well as teaching at Miss Wooler's school at Roe Head, she also worked as a governess for two families: in 1839 for three months for the Sidgwicks at Stonegappe in Lothersdale, and in 1841 for the White family in Rawdon. The position of governess was one of the only ways in which a woman of Charlotte's class could hope to earn a living in the nineteenth century, but it was often arduous and poorly paid work. Charlotte struggled to adapt to the role of governess and the hardships it frequently entailed.

The life of the governess was a lonely one: governesses ranked above the household servants, yet were not considered part of the family, nor likely to be treated as such. Such was Charlotte's experience with the Sidgwick family, as she detailed in a letter to her sister, Emily, concluding that a governess's lot is indeed a hard one: 'I see now more clearly than I have ever done before that a private governess has no existence, is not considered as a living and rational being except as connected with the wearisome duties she has to fulfil.' Mrs Sidgwick made no effort to befriend Charlotte, and was defensive when Charlotte complained of the children's behaviour. This attitude is replicated by the Ingram family in *Jane Eyre*. Blanche Ingram, Jane's rival for Rochester's affections, describes the governesses of her own childhood thus: 'half of them detestable and the rest ridiculous, and all incubi', while her mother declares, 'I have suffered a martyrdom from their incompetency and caprice.'

Blanche Ingram describes the tricks that she and her sister used to play on their governesses, and indeed in her own experience, Charlotte found the children to be as unwelcoming as their mother, referring to them in her letter to Emily as 'riotous, perverse, unmanageable cubs' and in a letter to Ellen as 'a set of pampered, spoilt, turbulent children, whom I was expected constantly to amuse, as well as to instruct'. It is here we find the originals of the spoilt and precocious children of Brontë's fiction – John Reed and his sisters, Adèle Varens (although the endearing Polly in *Villette* is probably a representation of Elizabeth Gaskell's daughter, Julia, to whom Charlotte became particularly attached on a visit to Gaskell and her family). Contemplating her future at the close of 1839, it is hardly surprising that she declares, 'I hate and abhor the very thoughts of governess-ship.' In a later letter to her publisher, she expounded on the difficulties of a governess's existence. She refers to 'a life of inexpressible misery' in which the governess was 'tyrannized over, finding her efforts to please and teach utterly vain, chagrined, distressed, worried – so badgered so trodden-on, that she ceased almost at last to know herself, and wondered in what despicable, trembling frame her oppressed mind was prisoned'. The letter is suggestive of the extent to which Charlotte felt she had lost her identity whilst working as a governess: once again, she had been forced to adopt a mask, to perform a role against which she inwardly railed.

Shortly after her return to Haworth following the conclusion of her employment with the Sidgwick family, Charlotte received a marriage proposal from Ellen Nussey's brother, Henry. Responding to his proposal, she writes: 'I have no personal repugnance to the idea of a union with you – but I feel convinced that mine is not the sort of disposition calculated to form the happiness of a man like you,' concluding, 'I will never for the sake of attaining the distinction of matrimony and escaping the stigma of an old maid take a worthy man whom I am conscious that I cannot render happy.' To Ellen, she confessed, 'I […] never could have that intense attachment which would make me willing to die for him – and if ever I marry it must be in that light of adoration that I will regard my Husband.' Charlotte was almost twenty-three when she received Henry's proposal of marriage: old enough to consider spinsterhood a distinct possibility in the nineteenth century. A few months later, she rejected another proposal of marriage, this time from the Reverend David Pryce, who, after meeting her once, wrote to her declaring his attachment and asking for her hand. It was hardly surprising, given their brief acquaintance, that she rejected his offer. Her account of this event to Ellen Nussey, however, suggests that she was resigned to, indeed even welcomed, the possibility of spinsterhood: 'I am certainly doomed to be an old maid,' she declared, continuing, 'Never mind. I made up my mind to that fate ever since I was twelve years old.' Her attitude towards marriage is reinforced in a later letter to Ellen Nussey, in which she declares,

> Not that it is a crime to marry – or a crime to wish to be married – but it is an imbecility which I reject with

contempt – for women [who] have neither fortune nor beauty – to make marriage the principal object of their wishes & hopes & the aim of all their actions – not to be able to convince themselves that they are unattractive – and that they had better be quiet and think of other things than wedlock.

Marriage was undoubtedly a problematic institution in the nineteenth century: for much of the period women retained barely any legal rights once married, effectively becoming the property of their husbands. Nevertheless, marriage offered the possibility of financial security and an escape from the drudgery of the life of a governess. Indeed, marriage, for many Victorian women, was not only desirable but essential: few women had the privilege of an independent income, and employment opportunities, for middle- and upper-class women in particular, were extremely limited. Romantic love was therefore frequently less of a consideration in the decision to marry than in today's world. Unmarried daughters were frequently perceived as a burden on their family, and would often be left to make their own way in the world in the event of their father's death (any inheritance generally passing to the eldest son). Cases of respectable, middle-class unmarried women finding themselves in the workhouse were not uncommon. When Charlotte rejected Henry Nussey, Patrick Brontë was already in his sixties, and she must have anticipated a time when she would not only be obliged to earn her own living, but to provide a roof over her head as well. Despite this, she appears at this period at least to have subscribed to a wholly romantic view of marriage, and to have dismissed the practical implications of spinsterhood, believing fervently that to marry without love would be inherently wrong (an attitude that anticipates the heroine's rejection of St John Rivers in *Jane Eyre*).

In a letter to Ellen Nussey from 1840, Charlotte clarified her views on marriage:

Do not be over-persuaded to marry a man you can never respect – I do not say love, because I think, if you can re-spect a person before marriage, moderate love at least will come after; and as to intense passion, I am convinced that that is no desirable feeling. In the first place, it seldom or never meets with a requital; and, in the second place, if it did, the feeling would only be temporary: it would last the honeymoon, and then, perhaps, give place to disgust, or indifference, worse perhaps than disgust. Certainly this would be the case on the man's part; and on the woman's – God help her, if she is left to love passionately and alone […] I am tolerably well convinced that I shall never marry at all.

The letter demonstrates an awareness of the potential dangers of marriage, particularly for a woman: divorce was all but impossi-ble to obtain, and in any case was widely perceived, in accordance with the teachings of the Bible, as contrary to God's will ('What […] God hath joined together, let no man put asunder.')[7] For Charlotte, it seems, the danger was hardly worth the risk, and she appeared resolved to remain, as she termed it, 'an old maid'. In *The Professor*, Frances Crimsworth declares, 'An old maid's life must doubtless be void and vapid,' yet despite the frustration Charlotte evidently felt with the life of a teacher or governess, she evidently preferred these options to the possibility of mar-riage to a man whom she did not love.

Charlotte's second stint as a governess began in March 1841, when she was aged twenty-four, and was hardly more success-ful than her first. Again she was made to feel like an outsider among both the servants of the house and her employers, com-plaining to Ellen, 'I find it so difficult to ask either servants or mistress for anything I want.' The children, too, were proving difficult for Charlotte to manage – at once over-indulged and over-familiar. Homesickness added to Charlotte's woes, though her employers at least allowed, indeed encouraged visits from Charlotte's friends and family. The homesickness and trouble-some children rendered the position of governess highly dis tasteful to Charlotte, while the long working hours left her with barely enough time to correspond with friends and family, let alone indulge her creative instincts and the literary ambitions that she still harboured. Charlotte's dislike of her work, but the compulsion she felt to undertake it, are indicative of the limited choices available to women seeking respectable work in the mid-nineteenth century. 'I have no natural knack for my vocation,' she wrote to Ellen Nussey. 'If teaching only – were requisite it would be smooth and easy – but it is the living in other people's houses – the estrangement from one's real character – the adop-tion of a cold, frigid – apathetic exterior that is painful.' As a gov-erness, Charlotte was again required to play a role, to disguise her true self behind a mask; while she welcomed the mask she would later adopt to disguise her identity as writer, the mask of governess, like that of teacher, was intolerable to her.

In response to the deep frustration and unhappiness she felt in her post as governess, Charlotte began seriously to con-sider the possibility of opening a school with her sisters. She left her position with the White family at the end of 1841 intending to pursue this plan, which would potentially offer a means of making money that was infinitely preferable to the work of a governess, and which would enable the family to remain to-gether. As part of this scheme, Charlotte resolved to improve the planned school's chances of success by spending some time on the continent, in order to develop her language skills. She decided on Brussels, and secured positions for herself and Emily as pupils at Madame Heger's *pensionnat*. Her experiences in Brussels, and in particular her relationship with Mme Heger's husband, Constantin, marked a pivotal period in her life, and one that was to exert a considerable influence on her fiction.

Charlotte and Emily arrived in Brussels in February 1842 and took up residence as pupils at the *pensionnat* – Charlotte returning to formal schooling at the age of twenty-five. A few months later, in a letter to Ellen Nussey, she detailed her first impressions of the school and its staff, revealing that she was vastly happier as a school pupil than she had been as a governess, despite being far from home and somewhat isolated as a Protestant amongst Catholics. Charlotte was somewhat suspicious of Catholicism, and a number of her letters are suggestive of distinctly anti-Catholic feelings (in a later letter to Ellen, she scathingly refers to Catholicism as 'a most feeble childish piece of humbug'). She also reveals in her letter to Ellen her first impressions of Constantin Heger. Though her description of him is far from suggestive of a romantic infatuation, his characteristics as described by Charlotte bear a resemblance to those of her later fictional heroes – *Jane Eyre*'s Rochester and *Villette*'s Paul Emanuel – and her lengthy discussion of his character is clearly suggestive of her developing feelings for him:

[H]e is a professor of Rhetoric a man of power as to mind but very choleric & irritable in temperament – a little, black, ugly being with 'a face' that varies in expression, sometimes he borrows the lineaments of an insane tom-cat – sometimes those of a delirious Hyena – occasionally – but very seldom he discards these perilous attractions and assumes an air not above a hundred degrees removed from what you would call mild & gentleman-like.

Compare this to Lucy Snowe's description of Paul Emanuel in *Villette*:

A dark little man he certainly was; pungent and austere. Even to me he seemed a harsh apparition, with his close-shorn, black head, his broad, sallow brow, his thin cheek, his wide and quivering nostril, his thorough glance and hurried bearing. Irritable he was; one heard that, as he apostrophised with vehemence the awkward squad under his orders.

There can be no doubt that Charlotte had in mind her former master when she created the character of Paul Emanuel, and the problematic heroes of her other novels undoubtedly also owe something to her attraction to M. Heger.

Charlotte appears to have settled reasonably well in Brussels. She strove hard to improve her language skills, and though she suffered some attacks of homesickness, they were not frequent or entirely unbearable – no doubt partly a result of the fact that Emily had accompanied her, while Mary Taylor and her sister were also resident in the city at this time. Hence she was not entirely removed from friends and family despite the unfamiliar setting. In the summer of 1842, the sisters accepted a proposal from Mme Heger to teach English and music at the school. Though the positions were unpaid, they were given free bed and board in return, as well as continued tuition in those areas in which they wished to improve themselves.

In November of that year, Charlotte and Emily received news of their Aunt Branwell's illness and subsequent death, and returned to Haworth immediately. Their aunt's death followed those of Mary Taylor's sister, Martha, and Patrick's assistant curate at Haworth, William Weightman, who had become a close family friend. '[H]ow dreary and void everything seems,' Charlotte wrote to Ellen in response to this spate of deaths – a terrible foreshadowing of the grief that was still to come. While the sisters were at Haworth, Constantin Heger wrote to Patrick Brontë expressing his regret at the circumstances that had called them home, and declaring a 'fatherly affection for them'. He talked positively of the sisters' progress, and of what might still be achieved were they to continue their studies. A short time later, and no doubt partly in response to Heger's letter, Charlotte once again set off for Brussels, this time alone (Emily remained at Haworth, unable to bear to be parted from the family and moors once again), to once more take up the position of teacher at Mme Heger's *pensionnat*.

Charlotte's solitary return to Brussels sparked speculation among some of her acquaintances regarding her motivation, and it was rumoured that she had a romantic interest there. She of course disputed this, but there can be little doubt that her return to Brussels was at least in part motivated by her feelings for M. Heger. In attempting to quash speculation about a possible forthcoming union, she declared to Ellen that she 'never exchange[s] a word with any other man than Monsieur Heger' – an assertion that takes on new significance in light of her later letters to her old master. However, though she was welcomed by the Hegers on her return, Charlotte's sense of isolation and homesickness developed over the coming months, becoming almost unbearable during the school's summer vacation, when she spent much of her time alone. Her feelings for Constantin Heger increased, and she experienced a growing sense of antipathy towards his wife. Upon Charlotte's return, Heger and his brother-in-law took English lessons with her: a reversal of their former pupil-teacher relationship, which is echoed in the shifting power relations between Charlotte's heroes and heroines in her novels. At the heart of much of her fiction is the question of power in the relationship between a man and a woman: Jane Eyre is Rochester's employee, and subsequently his wife, but there is a distinct shift in the relationship between them following the fire at Thornfield, which leaves Rochester blind and consequently dependent on Jane; in *Shirley*, Louis Moore is tutor to the wealthy eponymous heroine, but again the relationship is reversed when Shirley marries her former tutor at the conclusion of the novel; questions of power also pervade the relationship between Lucy Snowe and Paul Emanuel in *Villette*.

Her letters from the period of her second sojourn in Brussels hint at her increasing attraction to her employer; she makes frequent reference to trivial events that bring the two of them into contact, and hints at the possible suspicions of Mme Heger: in a letter to Emily, she writes, 'I am convinced she does not like me – why, I can't tell, nor do I think she herself has any definite reason for the aversion.' Later, to Ellen, she confesses, 'I fancy I begin to perceive the reason for this mighty distance and reserve.' Though she does not elaborate, there is a hint here that Mme Heger suspects that Charlotte's feelings towards her husband are more than they ought to be. In a later letter Charlotte writes of Mme Heger, 'I no longer trust her' – a feeling that was no doubt mutual.

Amidst increasing feelings of melancholy and homesickness, Charlotte strove to endure her time in Brussels. In spite of her tendency towards anti-Catholic sentiments, finding herself one day outside the Church of Ste Gudule, she entered and, apparently on a whim, visited the confessional. She details the event in a letter to Emily. The priest at first refused to allow her the privilege of confession, as she had admitted to him that she was in fact a Protestant. Eventually, however, he relented, and Charlotte tells her sister that, 'I actually did confess – a real confession.' She does not elaborate on the details of the confession, but it is possible that she admitted to the Catholic priest her feelings for Heger. Though she may have found the experience cathartic, she had no intention of considering a conversion to Catholicism, and is at pains to assure her sister of this, and for Emily to keep the anecdote from their father, lest he worry that she may be about to abandon her Protestant faith.

Though her letters from Brussels suggest that she often felt deeply unhappy there following her solitary return, she nevertheless refused to come home while she had no real plan of what she might do upon her return. Her reluctance to leave Brussels was undoubtedly increased by her continued attachment to Heger, though she must have realised that nothing could come of her feelings. Eventually, however, she felt that life in Brussels was no longer endurable, and took the decision to resign her post and return home. She informed Mme Heger of her decision, but, on M. Heger's hearing of it, he sent for her and insisted she remain, which, inevitably, she agreed to do – for the short term, at least. Two months later, however, in December 1843, she finally resolved to resign her post and return to her beloved Haworth, believing that her spirits might lift when she was once more among friends and family.

Charlotte left Brussels and arrived home in January 1844. Despite being reunited with family and home, and later that year with Ellen and Mary, the overwhelming feelings of depression and despair continued to plague her. In a surprisingly candid letter to Ellen Nussey, she hints strongly at her feelings for her former master and employer: 'I think however long I live I shall not forget what the parting with M. Heger cost me – It grieved me so much to grieve him who has been so true and kind and disinterested a friend.' Although she was now separated from Heger, her feelings for him remained unresolved, and over the next two years she wrote him a series of increasingly despairing letters, in which she makes little attempt to disguise her true feelings for him. An unspecified number of these letters have not survived. The earliest known surviving letter remains as a result of the apparently jealous behaviour of Mme Heger. The letter was ripped up and discarded by M. Heger, but subsequently retrieved and reassembled by his wife. The content of the letter suggests that Mme Heger's jealousy was not entirely without foundation, though there is no indication that Charlotte's feelings for M. Heger were reciprocated. She writes, 'I am quite convinced that I shall see you again one day – I don't know how or when – but it must happen since I so long for it.' She also discusses her desire to write a book and to dedicate it to Heger – 'the only master I have ever had'. She concludes the letter in a similar romantic fashion: 'It hurts to say goodbye even in a letter – Oh it is certain I shall see you again one day – it really has to be so.'

Further evidence of Charlotte's continued infatuation with Heger again comes courtesy of his wife, who sewed together the pieces of two subsequent letters that her husband had attempted to destroy. The first was written in October 1844, almost ten months after Charlotte's departure from Brussels. Having heard nothing from Heger for several months, despite writing to him

at least twice, she almost begs him to contact her: 'I am count-
ing on soon having news of you – this thought delights me.'
This letter too was to elicit no response, prompting her to write
yet again, in January 1845, her tone increasingly desperate: 'If
my master withdraws his friendship from me entirely I shall be
absolutely without hope – if he gives me a little friendship – a
very little – I shall be content – happy, I would have a motive for
living – for working.' Charlotte's final surviving letter to Heger
dates from November 1845 – almost two years after she had left
Brussels. Again, her infatuation shows no sign of abating. It
appears that Heger had written to Charlotte in response to her
previous letter, though his letter does not survive, and neither
does her initial reply, in which she apparently promised to write
only every six months, though she berates him for this: 'Imagine
for a moment that one of your children is separated from you
by a distance of 160 leagues, and that you have to let six months
go by without writing to him, without receiving news of him,
without hearing him spoken of, without knowing how he is.'
She continues, 'I have tried to forget you […] I have done everything, I have sought occupations, I have absolutely forbidden
myself the pleasure of speaking about you – even to Emily, but
I have not been able to overcome either my regrets or my impa-
tience.' The final part of her letter suggests that her feelings had
almost reached the point of obsession:

> Your last letter has sustained me – has nourished me for six
> months – now I need another and you will give it me […]
> To forbid me to write to you, to refuse to reply to me – that
> will be to tear from me the only joy I have on earth – to
> deprive me of my last remaining privilege – a privilege
> which I will never consent to renounce voluntarily. Believe
> me, my master, in writing to me you do a good deed – so
> long as I think you are fairly pleased with me, so long as
> I still have the hope of hearing from you, I can be tranquil
> and not too sad, but when a dreary and prolonged silence

seems to warn me that my master is becoming estranged from me – when day after day I await a letter and day after day disappointment flings me down again into overwhelming misery, when the sweet delight of seeing your writing and reading your counsel flees from me like an empty vision – then I am in a fever – I lose my appetite and my sleep – I pine away.

Whether Charlotte continued to write to her former master, or whether she finally accepted that he had no wish to continue their acquaintance, is unclear. Whatever the case may have been, her infatuation with Heger exerted a huge influence on her fiction: her portrayal of Rochester's unfortunate marriage to Bertha Mason in *Jane Eyre*, Bertha's subsequent death and Rochester's union with Jane may well have been rooted in her romantic fantasies of Heger and her jealousy of his wife; while her final novel, *Villette*, published nine years after she left Brussels, along with the first novel she wrote, *The Professor*, owe an obvious debt to her time in Brussels and her relationship with Heger.

While Charlotte agonised over her separation from and lack of contact with Heger, there was a new arrival at Haworth in the form of Patrick's newly appointed curate, Arthur Bell Nicholls, whom Charlotte would later marry. Nicholls arrived in Haworth in May 1845. Like Patrick Brontë, he was originally from what is now Northern Ireland. Charlotte's first impression was of 'a respectable young man' (Nicholls was three years her junior). The following year, Ellen Nussey reported to her friend a rumour that Charlotte was to marry her father's curate; Charlotte responded with disbelief:

[…] never was a rumour more unfounded […] I could by no means think of mentioning such a rumour to him even as a joke – it would make me the laughing-stock of himself and his fellow curates for half a year to come – They regard me as an old maid, and I regard them, one and all, as highly uninteresting, narrow and unattractive specimens of the 'coarser sex'.

Charlotte seems to have retained this impression of her father's curate for some time: the following year she wrote to Ellen declaring, 'I cannot for my life see those interesting germs of goodness in him you discovered, his narrowness of mind always strikes me chiefly – I fear he is indebted to your imagination for his hidden treasures.' Given her earlier assertion that she could only marry a man she truly loved, her view of Nicholls did not seem to make him a likely candidate for her future husband, yet such was to be the case.

As Charlotte battled with her feelings for Heger and attempted to dispel the rumours relating to her father's curate, her brother, Branwell, was fighting his own demons. Between 1840 and 1845, Branwell held a number of positions as he strove to carve out a successful career for himself. He remained optimistic about his chances of poetic success, encouraged by a meeting with Hartley Coleridge in 1840, but in the meantime he struggled to earn a living. He was dismissed from his post as tutor to the sons of Robert and Agnes Postlethwaite for reasons unknown (though Juliet Barker, in her biography of the Brontë family, speculates that he may have been involved in a sexual liaison with one of the servants, resulting in pregnancy), and again from his position as clerk at Luddenden Foot railway station in Calderdale in 1842 for carelessness, and subsequently appointed tutor to the Robinson family at Thorp Green, where Anne Brontë was working as governess. His appointment was to prove disastrous: in July 1845, he was fired – apparently as a consequence of his relationship with his employer's wife, Mrs Lydia Robinson. In his despair, he turned increasingly to drink and opium. Branwell, like Charlotte, retained literary ambitions but, despite the publication of a number of his poems in local newspapers in the 1840s, it was becoming increasingly evident that he was unlikely to succeed, not only in a literary career, but in any capacity, and he was becoming a significant burden on his family.

Publication

Charlotte's dreams of a literary career seemed almost as distant as her brother's following her return from Brussels: her weak eyesight prevented her from writing much at this time, and her plans for the future were vague. Shortly after she arrived home, she was offered a teaching position at a school in Manchester, with a substantial salary of one hundred pounds. However, concerns about her father's health led her to reject the offer: Patrick Brontë's eyesight was failing, and he was becoming increasingly reliant on his daughters for assistance with everyday tasks (in 1846, he would travel to Manchester with Charlotte for a cataract operation). Charlotte still retained hopes of being able to open a school with her sisters, and following her return she attempted to locate a small number of children who might board as pupils at the parsonage. In 1844, she drafted a prospectus for the proposed school, detailing the subjects to be offered: writing, arithmetic, history, grammar, geography, needle work, French, German, Latin, music and drawing. The range of subjects gives an indication of Charlotte's own accomplishments at a time when women's education was frequently extremely limited. However, the recruitment of pupils, despite Charlotte's best efforts, proved impossible: Haworth's relative isolation acted as an effective deterrent, and Charlotte and her sisters were eventually forced to abandon their plans.

In the autumn of 1845, Charlotte discovered a selection of poetry by her sister, Emily. In her later biographical notice of her sisters, written after their deaths, she reveals that she accidentally discovered the poems, and read them in secret, without Emily's consent. Recognising the quality of her sister's work, she persuaded her to consider publication, although Emily was initially reluctant: Charlotte recalls 'it took hours to reconcile her to the discovery I had made, and days to persuade her that such poems merited publication.' The incident is suggestive of an almost ruthless ambition on the part of Charlotte: the reading of private, personal work and her desire to make it public suggest her literary aspirations appear to have overridden her sister's desire for privacy. The anecdote seems ironic in light of Charlotte's later experiences, when she sought desperately to protect her own privacy and avoid the revelation of her true identity. Charlotte's enthusiasm for Emily's poems led Anne to volunteer a number of her own productions, and Charlotte then set about encouraging her two sisters to embark on a project to publish a collection of their poems. Despite Southey's advice, Charlotte still dreamed of poetic success. By this point, she had effectively abandoned her literary alliance with her brother, whose tendency towards drink and dissipation prevented him from fulfilling the earlier ambitions both he and his family harboured for him. Still hoping to fulfil her own literary ambitions, Charlotte now turned to her two younger sisters. Though she was close to her sisters, the earlier alliance with Branwell and Emily's close relationship with Anne must necessarily have affected Charlotte: on the one hand, this new alliance with her sisters brought Charlotte closer than she had yet been to her dream of literary success; on the other hand, it must have been tinged with pain, marking as it did the abandonment of her earlier hopes and dreams for Branwell and herself.

The three sisters, while anxious to see their poetic productions in print, were keen to preserve the secret of their authorship, and consequently adopted the pseudonyms of Currer, Ellis and Acton Bell – which had the advantage of concealing not only their true identities, but their gender as well, something that Charlotte was anxious to do. Writing her biographical notice for a new edition of *Wuthering Heights* and *Agnes Grey* shortly after the deaths of Emily and Anne, she explained the reasoning behind their choice of pseudonyms:

> [W]e did not like to declare ourselves women, because – without at that time suspecting that our mode of writing and thinking was not what is called 'feminine' – we had a vague impression that authoresses are liable to be looked on with prejudice; we had noticed how critics sometimes use for their chastisement the weapon of personality, and for their reward, a flattery, which is not true praise.

Charlotte's desire to be praised for the quality of her work rather than judged by attitudes towards the woman writer stayed with her throughout her literary career, and she remained anxious to retain the secret of her sex following the publication of her first two novels. Her anxiety was entirely justified. The woman poet, in particular, was frequently distinguished from the figure of the male poet by the title 'poetess'. Primarily domestic – wifely and maternal – concerns were considered suitable subjects for the woman poet. While the poetess who adhered to these conventions might achieve moderate success and recognition for her literary endeavours, she was unlikely to be classed alongside her male counterparts. The image of the woman poet as poetess diffused the threat she posed to both the male poet and the patriarchal structures of Victorian society, for it essentially ensured she remained in the feminine realm, even as she entered the public world of writing and publishing. The gender-ambiguous pseudonyms selected by the three sisters were thus useful tools.

The sisters' collection of poetry, simply entitled *Poems*, was published in May 1846 under the pseudonyms Currer, Ellis and Acton Bell – ranked, thus, in order of the sisters' ages. It was largely ignored by critics, though a few short reviews appeared in the magazines of the day. The anonymous reviewer in *The Critic* praised the work excessively, declaring:

> Amid the heaps of trash and trumpery in the shape of verses, which lumber the table of the literary journalist, this small book [...] has come like a ray of sunshine, gladdening the eye with present glory [...] Here we have [...] original thoughts, expressed in the true language of poetry.

The Athenaeum was more qualified in its praise, suggesting that the three poets were of differing quality, citing Ellis as the most talented of the three, Acton as the weakest, and Currer as occupying the middle ground between these two. Though she was anxious for her sisters' as well as her own success, such a judgment may well have pained Charlotte. She had long harboured poetic aspirations, and the publication of the collection was largely due to her own exertions in persuading her sisters to agree to the project. To have her own work disparaged, albeit only slightly, in comparison with her younger sister's must surely have rankled somewhat. Nevertheless, in her discussion of the small volume of poetry in her biographical note for *Wuthering Heights* and *Agnes Grey*, the critics' view of the work seems to coincide with her own: 'all of it that merits to be known', she wrote, 'are the poems of Ellis Bell.' Subsequent critical assessment of the Brontë sisters' poetry has tended to agree with this view. It is significant, however, that the biographical note was written by Charlotte Brontë, the *novelist*, who had long since accepted that her literary success would not come in the form of poetry, and who had perhaps accepted her younger sister's greater poetic talent.

Though the volume received little attention in the press, the pseudonyms nevertheless sparked interest among those who did review the book as to the true identities of the poets – despite the fact that pseudonymous and anonymous publication was relatively common practice at the time. *The Athenaeum* assumed the collection to be the work of three brothers – an assumption that would no doubt have pleased Charlotte. W.A. Butler, writing in *Dublin University Magazine*, also seems to have taken it for granted that the poems were male-authored, though speculates that they may be the work of 'but one master spirit'. Such speculation was to continue for some time to come, particularly following the publication of the sisters' first novels. It was to prove particularly frustrating for Charlotte, who sought both to protect the identity of her sex, and to establish her work independently from that of her sisters.

Despite one or two positive reviews, the first edition of *Poems* by Currer, Ellis and Acton Bell (a print run of one thousand) had sold only two copies a year after its first appearance. Nevertheless, Charlotte continued to pursue her dreams of poetic success, and resolved to send a number of the unsold copies to some of the most famous writers of the day, repeating the experiment undertaken by herself and Branwell ten years earlier. The recipients of this gesture included Wordsworth, Tennyson and Hartley Coleridge (Southey, whose words of discouragement Brontë had ultimately chosen to ignore, had died some years earlier). The letters offering the gift of the volume of poetry are mockingly self-disparaging in tone, informing the correspondent that 'My relatives Ellis and Acton Bell and myself, heedless of the repeated warnings of various respectable publishers, have committed the rash act of printing a volume of poems.' However, the gift of the volume to the various writers of the day suggests that Charlotte retained at least some hope that the poetic talents of the Bells would be recognised. This was not to be, and, though the poetry of Charlotte and her sisters has received subsequent critical attention, their success was to come as novelists rather than poets.

Charlotte's earlier letters and attempts to succeed as a poet suggest that, in her youth at least, she ranked poetry above novels in terms of literary greatness. This is particularly evident in a letter written to Ellen Nussey in which she responds to her friend's request to recommend some books for her perusal. Listing a number of poets, including Milton, Shakespeare, Byron, Wordsworth and Southey, she continues, 'For fiction, read Scott alone; all novels after his are worthless.' Her stance reflects broader attitudes towards literature, particularly in the first half of the nineteenth century, when the novel was persistently viewed as inferior to poetry.

Though Charlotte had harboured dreams of poetic success for many years, she had also been engaged in storytelling from her childhood, and the decision she now took to pursue a career as a novelist, though it in some respects may be perceived as a business decision, was nevertheless one with which she was more than comfortable as a writer. Hence, following the relative failure of the small volume of poetry, the sisters turned their attention to novel writing. In 1846, having completed their first novels (Charlotte's *The Professor*, Emily's *Wuthering Heights* and Anne's *Agnes Grey*), they began to approach publishers with a view to securing publication. They met with several rejections before Thomas Newby agreed to publish *Wuthering Heights* and *Agnes Grey*, on the proviso that the authors contributed towards the cost of publication. Charlotte, however, could find no one willing to publish *The Professor*. This rejection must have pained Charlotte deeply: as we have seen, from childhood she had aligned herself with Branwell, and Emily with Anne. By this time, Branwell's lifestyle could no longer be excused as mere youthful exuberance, and the family's hopes for the only son were effectively dashed. The literary alliance formed by Charlotte and Branwell had come to nothing, and the rejection of *The Professor* must have further increased Charlotte's sense of failure in light of her sisters' moderate success (though Newby's terms were far from favourable).

Charlotte did not, however, despair, and worked fervently on a new project – a three-volume novel which she hoped would meet with greater success than its predecessor. Meanwhile, she continued to submit *The Professor* to various publishing houses, though she had more or less resigned herself to rejection. She was therefore delighted when she received a detailed response from the publishers Smith, Elder and Co., who, while declining to publish her novel, nevertheless recognised her potential, and invited her to submit a three-volume work for their consideration. Charlotte, in due course, sent them the manuscript of *Jane Eyre*. Writing his memoirs over fifty years later, George Smith recalled the first impression the work made on him:

> After breakfast on Sunday morning I took the [manuscript] of 'Jane Eyre' to my little study, and began to read it. The story quickly took me captive. Before twelve o'clock my horse came to the door, but I could not put the book down [...] Presently the servant came to tell me that luncheon was ready; I asked him to bring me a sandwich and a glass of wine, and still went on with 'Jane Eyre' [...] [B]efore I went to bed that night I had finished reading the manuscript.[8]

Unsurprisingly, given this response, Smith, Elder and Co. agreed to the publication of *Jane Eyre*. They proved to be far more scrupulous publishers than Newby, who had taken no steps towards publishing *Wuthering Heights* and *Agnes Grey* since his initial acceptance. It was therefore *Jane Eyre* that appeared first, in October 1847, with Charlotte once again adopting the pseudonym Currer Bell. The novel proved an instant success, selling widely and attracting the attention of both periodicals and the major writers of the day: it was the subject of endless column inches in the press over the coming months, as speculation mounted as to the identity, and in particular the sex, of the author, and debate over the morality of the tale raged.

Charlotte took an avid interest in the critics' responses to her first published novel. Most were positive: the critic in *The Atlas*, for example, declared it to be 'not merely a work of great promise; it is one of absolute performance', while *The Critic*, which had sung the praises of *Poems*, described it as 'a remarkable novel, in all respects very far indeed above the average of those which the literary journalist is doomed every season to peruse'. *Jane Eyre* was not without its critics, however, and Charlotte was particularly alert to criticisms of her writing, her long-cherished desire for literary success perhaps making her feel such things more keenly than most. For the rest of her life, she was to take criticism of her work to heart. The central accusation levelled at *Jane Eyre* involved the issue of morality. Given the novel's content, and the Victorian sense of propriety, this is, perhaps, hardly surprising: Charlotte's 'hero', Rochester, is far from the masculine ideal, though he may be a more realistic representative of the Victorian gentleman than many other literary heroes of the time. He openly admits to an illicit relationship with a French actress, through which he may or may not have fathered an illegitimate child; he attempts to dupe the heroine into a bigamous marriage, before trying to convince her to live as his mistress; and for all this he is apparently rewarded at the conclusion of the novel with a happy marriage to the heroine. While the image of the Victorians as bastions of purity, morality and propriety is far from an accurate one, it has emerged in part as a consequence of the image of itself that Victorian society wished to project. Novels, according to the moralists of the day, should reflect this sense of morality – particularly novels that were likely to be read by ladies. Fiction that suggested that the upper and middle classes were less than virtuous was distinctly unwelcome in certain quarters of society, and this is reflected in some of the reviews of *Jane Eyre*.

A number of reviewers highlighted the questionable morality of the novel, while refraining from outright condemnation. Elizabeth Rigby, however, writing in the *Quarterly Review*, was deeply critical of the morality of *Jane Eyre*, suggesting that its popularity was due to its vulgarity, rather than its literary merit, and accusing the author of committing a great offence in her characterisation of Rochester – intended to appeal to the reader in spite of the fact that he 'is a man who deliberately and secretly seeks to violate the laws both of God and man'. She was similarly critical of the character of the heroine, accusing her of 'pedantry, stupidity, [and] gross vulgarity'. She declared the novel 'an anti-Christian composition', and accused it of 'moral, religious and literary deficiencies'. While such criticism undoubtedly stung, the anonymous review did not appear until December 1848; hence its effect on the author of *Jane Eyre* was tempered by the recent deaths of Branwell and Emily. Nevertheless, Charlotte would return to the review while writing *Shirley*, and responded specifically to Rigby's criticisms in a Preface written for her second novel.

As well as the perceived questionable morality of Charlotte's novel, a number of reviewers (Elizabeth Rigby amongst them) criticised the improbable and sensational aspects of the tale. Such assertions are, in many ways, justified, though this is not necessarily a criticism of the novel, and indeed the somewhat sensational plot has no doubt contributed to the ongoing popularity of *Jane Eyre*. The mid-nineteenth century, however, was the age of the realist novel, and *Jane Eyre*'s engagement with this genre is, to say the least, problematic: realist elements combine with the sensational and the supernatural, and for some readers these contrasting features sit uneasily alongside one another. While a number of reviewers praised Charlotte's characterisation, they questioned the more sensational aspects of the plot: H.F. Chorley, writing in *The Athenaeum*, concluded, 'we think the heroine too outrageously tried, and too romantically assisted in her difficulties,' while G.H. Lewes suggested that it contained 'too much melodrama and improbability, which smack of the circulating-library'. Such criticisms had a significant effect on Charlotte Brontë and her writing. Ever-conscious of her critics, she attempted, not entirely successfully, to address some of these concerns in her next novel, *Shirley*.

While reviewers debated the merits of *Jane Eyre*, there was also, continued and fevered speculation as to the identity of the author, much of which focused, to Charlotte's dismay, on the gender of the writer. Reviewers were divided over the question of the sex of the author: *The Examiner* declared that 'Though relating to a woman, we do not believe [*Jane Eyre*] to have been written by a woman,' while the reviewer in *Era* asserted even more vehemently, 'No woman could have penned [...] Jane Eyre.' G.H. Lewes, writing in *Fraser's Magazine*, disagreed, declaring 'The writer is evidently a woman.' *The Christian Remembrancer* agreed with Lewes, stating 'we [...] cannot doubt that the book is written by a female,' and Thackeray echoed this sentiment in a private letter, though noting that the author 'knows her language better than most ladies do'. The questionable morality of Charlotte's characters, and particularly Rochester, might be partially excused if the author was a man; should the author prove to be a woman, however, her knowledge of such things would be considered shocking in certain sections of society. Again, Charlotte's concern, undoubtedly, was to try and ensure that her work was judged on its literary merits, rather than on the sex of its author. Discussing the speculation in a letter to her publishers, she wrote, 'To such critics I would say – "to you I am neither Man nor Woman – I come before you as an Author only – it is the sole standard by which you have a right to judge me – the sole ground on which I accept your judgement."' She was all too aware, though, that such protestations would not be heeded.

After witnessing the success of *Jane Eyre*, Newby finally published *Wuthering Heights* and *Agnes Grey*. There was immediate speculation as to the relationship between the authors of these novels and the author of *Jane Eyre*. Rumour suggested that Currer, Ellis and Acton Bell were one and the same person, and that *Agnes Grey* and *Wuthering Heights* were the early productions of the author of *Jane Eyre*. Charlotte was anxious to dispel this myth – an anxiety probably at least partly rooted in the public response to *Wuthering Heights* in particular: if *Jane Eyre* could be accused of coarseness, it was nothing to Emily's novel, with its portrayal of the passionate, seemingly demonic Heathcliff. Reviewers described him as 'an incarnation of evil qualities' and 'a creature in whom every evil passion seems to have reached a gigantic excess', and the novel as a whole was deemed to be coarse and vulgar. Deeply concerned as she was with the criticism of *Jane Eyre*, Charlotte was less than desirous to have *Wuthering Heights* attributed to her as well. In December 1847, shortly after the publication of her sisters' novels, she wrote to her publisher, declaring – perhaps disingenuously – 'I should not be ashamed to be considered the author of "Wuthering Heights" and "Agnes Grey", but possessing no real claim to that honour, I would rather not have it attributed to me, thereby depriving the true authors of their just meed.' Nevertheless, speculation as to the identity of the Bell 'brothers', and rumours that the authors of the three novels were in fact one and the same person, continued to circulate.

In June the following year, T.C. Newby published Anne Brontë's second novel, *The Tenant of Wildfell Hall*. Through the experiences of her heroine, Helen Graham, Anne Brontë explores the issues of women's role within marriage and the effects of dissipation on the character of the husband (Arthur Huntingdon – influenced partly by Branwell Brontë), portraying the wife of an intemperate and adulterous husband who flees the marital home in order to protect her child. Inevitably, given the Victorian sense of propriety, as well as widespread attitudes towards the sanctity of marriage, the book provoked intense criticism, and Charlotte herself disapproved of her sister's choice of subject matter. Reviewers declared it to be 'repulsive', 'coarse' and 'disgusting', and *Sharpe's London Magazine* was anxious to dissuade its 'lady-readers' from reading it. Undoubtedly partly as a consequence of such reviews, Charlotte became even more anxious to disassociate herself from her sisters' work, and to prove the separate identities of Currer, Ellis and Acton Bell. The speculation that they were one and the same was given fresh impetus by Anne and Emily's publisher, Thomas Newby, who had written to an American publisher informing them that, 'to the best of his belief "Jane Eyre" "Wuthering Heights" – "Agnes Grey" – and "The Tenant of Wildfell Hall" [...] were all the production of one writer,' no doubt an attempt to increase the sales of Anne and Emily's works, which had proved far less popular with the reading public than *Jane Eyre*.

In an attempt to contradict Newby's assertion, Anne and Charlotte travelled to London shortly after the publication of *The Tenant of Wildfell Hall* to meet with Charlotte's publishers, George Smith and William Smith Williams. The two parties had never previously met, and up until this point Smith and Williams were unsure of the identity of the author of *Jane Eyre*. In meeting with her publishers, Charlotte not only proved the separate identities of the Bells, but also confirmed suspicions that Currer Bell was a woman. In doing so, she also confirmed suspicions that Currer Bell was a woman. Her publishers offered to introduce Charlotte to key figures on the literary scene – including G.H. Lewes, with whom Charlotte had corresponded, and Thackeray whom she had long admired and to whom she dedicated the second edition of *Jane Eyre*. Charlotte, however, remained anxious to preserve the secret of her identity, and in particular the secret of her sex, and hence refused these invitations, informing her publisher that 'to all the rest of the world we must be "gentlemen" as heretofore.' Though the sisters took a risk in travelling to London and revealing their identities to Charlotte's publishers, their secret remained concealed from the general public at least: 'What author,' she wrote to her publisher sometime later, 'would be without the advantage of being able to walk invisible?' As a child, her father had encouraged her to speak the truth from behind a mask; in youth, she had concealed her imaginary world from all but those closest to her; now, as a successful author, the desire to write from behind a mask of anonymity still prevailed.

Nevertheless, her willingness to risk the revelation of her identity seems indicative: perhaps she felt secure that she could continue to conceal her sex from the wider public, or perhaps her keenness to establish her individual identity as an author overrode her concerns that her gender would become known. Significantly, even after the trip to London, she continued to refer to Currer, Ellis and Acton Bell as men in her correspondence with her publishers, as though keen to preserve the facade even when they were fully aware of the truth (the incongruity is comical at times – her description of Acton Bell attending to his sewing at the fireside, for example).

Though Charlotte had taken steps to assure her publishers that the Bell 'brothers' were three separate writers, she remained anxious to disassociate herself from her sisters' work. Discussing Anne's second novel in her correspondence with her publisher following her return from London, she refrained from overt criticism, merely describing the subject as 'unfortunately chosen'. However, she was clearly piqued by William Smith Williams' reply, in which he compared Arthur Huntingdon to Rochester. She responded with barely concealed frustration, 'there is no likeness between the two; the foundation of each character is entirely different.' Huntingdon she considered to be 'a specimen of the naturally selfish sensual, superficial man', while Rochester, she insisted, 'has a thoughtful nature and a very feeling heart'; Heathcliff, meanwhile, she condemns as 'a mere demon'. Despite these assertions, there *are* significant parallels between the male protagonists of the Brontë novels, who all, to varying degrees, deviate from the image of the Victorian masculine ideal. While Arthur Huntingdon's tendency towards dissipation and adultery, and his treatment of his wife, may mark him out as a villainous character, and Heathcliff's all-consuming desire for revenge makes him something of an unsympathetic figure, the characters of Rochester, Robert Moore (*Shirley*) and Gilbert Markham (*The Tenant of Wildfell Hall*), with whom the reader is encouraged to identify, are all problematic figures: Rochester's illicit affair with Adèle's mother, attempts to dupe the heroine into a bigamous marriage, and imprisonment of his first wife represent potential dilemmas for the modern feminist reader at least; Robert Moore is willing to enter into a mercenary marriage with the eponymous heroine, before he is eventually united with Caroline Helstone; and Gilbert Markham, spoilt and indulged by his mother, repeatedly exhibits a desire to control the heroine, Helen Graham, suggesting parallels with the novel's villain, Arthur Huntingdon. These characters are thus not as dissimilar as Charlotte may have desired or claimed.

Though responses to the three novels caused moments of concern for Charlotte, she must nevertheless have delighted in her newfound success. After years of struggling to fulfil her literary ambitions while enduring the monotonous life of a teacher and governess, she finally succeeded, with the publication of *Jane Eyre*, in obtaining the goal she had so long desired – earning both a living and a reputation through her writing. While the struggle between the duties of the teacher/governess and the ambitions of the writer was now effectively over, Charlotte would continue to experience an intense sense of conflict in her life, as she struggled to preserve the secret of her true identity, despite the success of her works. The mask of Currer Bell was beginning to slip, and rumours began to spread among her friends and acquaintances that she had written a novel, though she endeavoured to keep her authorship of *Jane Eyre* from all but those closest to her; indeed, even Branwell and, for some time, Ellen and her father, were unaware of Currer Bell's true identity. When rumour reached Ellen that Charlotte had penned a novel, she was reprimanded for crediting such rumours: 'I have given no one a right either to affirm, or hint, in the most distant manner, that I am "publishing" [...] Though twenty books were ascribed to me, I should own none. I scout the idea utterly.' This statement, which amounts to little less than a barefaced lie, may have its origins in Anne's, and particularly Emily's reluctance to reveal their identities as the Bell 'brothers', but there can be no doubt that Charlotte too remained anxious to preserve the secret for as long as possible. However, although the rumours that circulated proved a source of deep frustration for Charlotte, her greatest struggle was yet to come. Though Anne had already published her second novel, Charlotte cannot have imagined the grief with which she would have to contend before the work on which she was now engaged saw the light of day.

Bereavement

While Charlotte was still flush with the success of *Jane Eyre*, and working earnestly on her next novel, she experienced the first of the three tragic losses that were to befall her in quick succession in the coming months. Following the publication of *Jane Eyre*, life at the parsonage had grown ever more difficult as a consequence of Branwell's continued decline. He became increasingly reliant on alcohol following his dismissal from the Robinson household, funding his habit by begging his father for money or incurring debts that his father was then forced to pay. In 1846, his former employer, Mr Robinson, died. Branwell professed to have hoped that such an event might clear the way for a union with his former mistress. However, following Mr Robinson's death, Branwell claimed that his marriage to Lydia Robinson was prevented by a clause in her husband's will that threatened to disinherit her if she saw her former lover again (an anecdote that seems to anticipate Casaubon's treatment of Dorothea in George Eliot's *Middlemarch*). There was no such clause, although whether or not Branwell was aware of this is unclear. Nevertheless, the incident seemed to plunge him further into despair, for which he continued to seek solace in drink and drugs.

Charlotte witnessed her brother's decline and the destruction of the family's hopes for him with an increasing sense of frustration and despair. If she empathised in any way with his apparent unrequited love for Lydia Robinson, in light of her own feelings for M. Heger, she had no sympathy or respect for his manner of dealing with it, having herself largely internalised her unhappiness at the separation from Heger. Branwell's letters suggest a distinct tendency towards melancholy, pessimism and despair: disappointed in love, he refused to pursue his dream of a literary career, believing that his work would merely be overlooked by publishers and libraries, and referring to his inability to write whilst suffering 'from agony to which the grave would be far preferable'. This sense of hopelessness prevailed for the rest of his life, as he increasingly sought solace in alcohol and opium: 'If I sit down and try to write,' he wrote to a friend in 1847, 'all ideas that used to come clothed in sunlight now press round me in funeral black; for really every pleasurable excitement that I used to know has changed to insipidity or pain.' Fearful of inflicting further pain on their already suffering brother, Charlotte and her sisters refrained from telling him of their own literary successes, and he was to die unaware that all three of them were published authors.

Following Branwell's further deterioration in the wake of Robinson's death, Charlotte described his behaviour as 'intolerable': 'he is continually screwing money out of [Papa] sometimes threatening to kill himself if it is withheld from him [...] [H]e will do nothing – except drink, and make us all wretched.' Branwell's gradual decline had a significant effect on his immediate family: not only was he a financial burden, with his refusal to work and his constant demands for money, but his descent into alcohol and drug abuse also marked the destruction of the hopes that the family had invested in him for so long. Branwell himself acknowledged this, admitting the year before he died that, 'I shall never be able to realize the too sanguine hopes of my friends.' In a letter to Ellen Nussey (whose own brother Joseph appears to have been a similar burden on his family, and, like Branwell, died young), Charlotte described her brother as 'a drain on every resource – an impediment to all happiness'. Given the pair's childhood alliance and shared dreams of literary success, Branwell's tendency towards self-destruction must have been particularly painful for Charlotte. As it became apparent that Branwell would not fulfil these ambitions, Charlotte's own recent success as a writer must have been tinged with sadness and regret at what might have been for the brother who showed so much promise in his youth.

Branwell's lifestyle took an inevitable toll on his health. He had trouble sleeping and grew gradually more wasted in appearance. Though it was apparent to all that his health was failing, the suddenness with which death eventually overtook him came as something of a shock. On 22nd September 1848, he was still able to make the short walk into Haworth; the following day it became clear that he was seriously ill and he was confined to bed. The day after, with his family at his bedside, he died, at the age of just thirty-one. Despite the earlier losses of her mother, sisters and aunt, Branwell's was the first death that Charlotte witnessed directly. Though she found the scene painful in the extreme, and though undoubtedly grieved at her brother's death at such an early age, she was far from devastated by his loss: indeed, in light of his final years of decline and misery, his death seems to have come as something of a relief. She mourned not the loss of life, but the waste of talent: 'I had aspirations and ambitions for him once,' she wrote to William Smith Williams. These aspirations were the same as those she cherished for herself; while experiencing the fulfilment of her own ambitions, she was forced to come to terms with the utter destruction of Branwell's. It was perhaps this, as well as the painful memories of his final years, that contributed to her own ill health immediately following her brother's death: she was overcome with 'heartache and sickness' and eventually fever. She was confined to bed, and the doctor called in to advise. Though she recovered, she remained ill for several weeks after Branwell's death, and the immediacy of her loss, as well as her own delicate health, had a detrimental effect on her ability to write; her imagination, she declared, was rendered 'pale, stagnant, mute'. Though in many ways she sought to separate her public self as writer from her private self as sister and daughter, this proved all but impossible, and again and again in the months that followed her imagination seemed to stagnate as she sought to deal with the loss of those she loved. *Shirley*, on which she had begun working a few months earlier, was put to one side; by the time she returned to it, she was the solitary survivor of the six children of Patrick and Maria Brontë.

While Branwell's death eventually came as something of a relief for Charlotte, the losses that she was to experience so soon afterwards were to prove devastating. Writing to Ellen of her brother's death in October 1848, Charlotte informed her that 'Emily and Anne are pretty well – though Anne is always delicate, and Emily has a cold & cough at present.' Emily's apparently trivial symptoms were eventually to prove fatal: unbeknown to the grieving sisters, she was already suffering from the disease from which she would die only two months later. Emily's cough remained with her, and towards the end of October, Charlotte grew concerned: these symptoms were now accompanied by a shortness of breath, and the deterioration of her health grew increasingly obvious from her appearance. She was, in fact, suffering from tuberculosis – the disease that had already claimed the lives of three of Charlotte's siblings. Emily had, since childhood, exhibited a degree of obstinacy, and she refused now to acknowledge that her symptoms were indicative of any serious illness, rejecting offers of remedies and medical advice, much to her family's frustration. Furthermore, while Emily's health steadily deteriorated, Charlotte grew increasingly concerned about Anne's delicate health, though she initially attempted to dismiss her fears regarding her sisters as a reaction to Branwell's death. To add to her woes, her father, their beloved servant Tabby, and Ellen Nussey were also suffering from ill health at this time. Charlotte was thus plagued with uncertain fears: 'Without health,' she wrote to her publisher, 'there is little comfort.' While the health of others improved, Emily's continued to deteriorate. Her stoicism in the face of illness made it impossible at times for Charlotte to detect whether or not her health improved, but what hope there was ultimately proved false. Charlotte's letters from this time indicate the depth of her attachment to Emily, to whom she had grown closer as her relationship with Branwell had deteriorated: 'When she is ill,' she wrote to William Smith Williams, 'there seems to be no sunshine in the world for me; the tie of a sister is near and dear indeed.' Charlotte's relatively sheltered life and her small circle of acquaintances outside of her immediate family rendered her siblings of particular importance to her; the loss of Emily and Anne was all the more painful, in spite of any earlier sibling rivalry, because they had shared with her the fulfilment of her dream of becoming a writer. Over the course of her adult life, she had grown increasingly attached to Emily in particular, with whom she was closer in age, and with whom she had spent a significant amount of time in Brussels, removed from all other family members. The possibility of Emily's death was thus inexpressibly painful to her: 'I think Emily seems the nearest thing to my heart in this world,' she wrote, less than a month before her sister's death, and, a few days later, 'I must hope – she is dear to me as life.'

By late November, Emily's deterioration was apparent, yet she would consent to neither remedies nor medical advice, persistently ignoring the signs that indicated the severity of her illness. A mere ten days before her death, she was still refusing medical attention, though she did eventually agree to try some homeopathic remedies. By this time, however, intervention was useless. Indeed, given the mortality rates for tuberculosis in the nineteenth century, it seems unlikely that earlier intervention would have affected the outcome of the disease (certainly it proved worthless in the case of Anne Brontë just a few months later). Emily died on 19th December 1848, at the age of thirty, and was interred next to her mother, her sisters Maria and Elizabeth, and her brother in the church next to the parsonage where she had resided for most of her life. Charlotte's anguish at the loss of her dearest sister was acute, but barely had she had time to grieve, before it became apparent that Anne too was falling seriously ill.

While Charlotte still fluctuated between hope and despair over Emily, Anne was already showing signs of infection. In a letter written shortly before Emily's death, Charlotte refers to the pain that Anne suffered in her side – an indication that tuberculosis had already taken hold. Though Charlotte may have felt closer to Emily, Anne was now her only remaining sibling. William Smith Williams encouraged her to seek comfort from her last surviving sister through their shared sorrow, little imagining that Anne too would be lost to Charlotte within a few short months, and his letter thus takes on an additional sense of pathos and tragedy: 'You and your sister must be more & more endeared to each other now that you are left alone on earth, and having the same hopes, & sorrows, & pursuits, your sympathies will be more & more closely entwined.'

Anne's health deteriorated gradually but steadily over the coming months. Unlike Emily, she agreed to receive medical advice, but it was ultimately to no avail. In May 1849, Charlotte and Ellen Nussey accompanied Anne to Scarborough, in the hope that the sea air might improve her condition. It was not to be. Weakened by the slow but steady progress of the disease, she finally succumbed, dying peacefully at Scarborough on 28th May 1849, aged just twenty-nine, with Ellen and her one remaining sibling at her side. Unable to face the prospect of returning her sister's body to Haworth, Charlotte arranged for Anne to be buried in Scarborough, hence she is the only one of the Brontë family not interred in the family vault beneath the church in Haworth. Her funeral was attended by Charlotte, Ellen and Miss Wooler. Charlotte remained in the area with Ellen for a number of days following Anne's burial, before finally returning alone to Haworth and her grieving father.

Within the space of a few short months, the Brontë family had been devastated. Though Anne was the last and the youngest of her siblings to perish, Charlotte seems to have felt the loss of Emily more keenly. Three months after Emily's death, she declared, 'The feeling of Emily's loss does not diminish as time wears on.' Following Anne's death, she wrote to William Smith Williams of her loss: '[Anne's] quiet – Christian death did not rend my heart as Emily's stern, simple, undemonstrative end did – I let Anne go to God and felt He had a right to her. I could hardly let Emily go – I wanted to hold her back then – and I want her back now.'

Life at the parsonage following the death of Charlotte's siblings was desolate, and the last surviving sibling's grief at the loss of her family is palpable in her letters from this period. Addressing her publisher shortly after the death of her sister Anne, she refers to her recent losses: 'They are both gone – and so is poor Branwell – and Papa has now me only – the weakest – puniest – least promising of his six children.' Though Charlotte found solace in her faith following her siblings' deaths, she nevertheless struggled to reconcile herself to the life of solitude that now lay before her. Her letters from this period refer to the monotony of her existence, and it is clear that she suffered from frequent and extended bouts of depression. However, the process of completing her next novel proved a cathartic one, writing assisting in assuaging her grief somewhat. She completed the manuscript by early September, and *Shirley* was published at the end of October 1849.

Shirley is an uneven, at times disjointed novel, arguably suffering from the influence on the author of two crucial events – one public, one deeply personal: the critical reception of *Jane Eyre*, and the deaths of Branwell, Emily and Anne. Stung by some of the criticisms of *Jane Eyre*, Charlotte took pains to try and improve herself as a writer with her next novel. The opening chapter of *Shirley* can be seen as a direct response to the accusations of melodrama and sensationalism that were levelled at *Jane Eyre*. Addressing the reader directly, the narrator proceeds:

If you think […] that anything like a romance is preparing for you, reader, you never were more mistaken. Do you anticipate sentiment, and poetry, and reverie? Do you expect passion, and stimulus, and melodrama? Calm your expectations; reduce them to a lowly standard. Something real, cool, and solid lies before you.

While the first chapter certainly proceeds in this vain, satirically portraying three curates, who ultimately play only a minor role in the novel, overall the assertions made in the opening of the novel are not borne out by the remainder of the text, which details the experiences of the two heroines, Caroline Helstone and Shirley Keeldar, their romantic attachments, and their proximity to the Luddite disturbances of the early nineteenth century. While *Shirley* is less sensational than *Jane Eyre* in many respects, like its predecessor it combines realism with romance, and these two elements of the text do not always sit comfortably with one another.

Brontë's attempt to use her second published novel as a vehicle to respond to criticisms of *Jane Eyre* is also evident in the Preface she wished to include, a direct response to Elizabeth Rigby's critical review of *Jane Eyre*. Like the first chapter of *Shirley*, the intended Preface, entitled 'A Word to the Quarterly', is satirical in tone, yet the bitterness Brontë felt towards reviewers such as Rigby is evident: she concludes the Preface by advising her addressee 'to turn out and be a governess yourself for a couple of years – the experiment would do you good: [...] two years of uncheered solitude might perhaps teach you that to be callous, harsh and unsympathising is not to be firm, superior and magnanimous'. Unsurprisingly, Brontë's publishers refused to include the Preface, and she, in turn, refused to supply an alternative, declining either to reveal her true identity or to allude to her recent losses.

Shirley is also somewhat problematic in terms of its social commentary. It is ostensibly concerned with both class and gender issues, but Brontë's engagement with these topics is far from straightforward. The novel was published a year after the Chartist disturbances of 1848, at a time when the issue of the rights of the working classes was a topic of much public debate and concern. However, while Elizabeth Gaskell's *Mary Barton*, which was published the year before *Shirley* and with which there were inevitable comparisons, is set in the 1830s and 1840s, hence dealing directly with contemporary concerns about class uprising, Brontë elected to set her novel in the early years of the nineteenth century; thus she deals not with the issues surrounding the Chartist movement, but with the Luddite disturbances of the 1810s. The narrative's social commentary in respect of class is therefore diluted by its historical focus.

The novel's concern with the role of women in society is also problematic. Discussing possible topics for her follow-up to *Jane Eyre*, Charlotte wrote to William Smith Williams in a letter that reveals something of her rather ambiguous views on the emerging feminist movement:

> I often wish to say something about the 'condition of women' question [...] It is true enough that the present market for female labour is quite overstocked – but where or how could another be opened? Many say that the professions now filled only by men should be open to women also – but are not their present occupants and candidates more than numerous enough to answer every demand? Is there any room for female lawyers, female doctors, female engravers, for more female artists, more authoresses? One can see where the evil lies – but who can point out the remedy? When a woman has a little family to rear and educate and a household to conduct, her hands are full, her vocation is evident – when her destiny isolates her – I suppose she must do what she can – live as she can – complain as little – bear as much – work as well as possible.

This ambiguity regarding a woman's right to work manifests itself in *Shirley*. Like her creator, Caroline Helstone suffers from bouts of melancholy, brought on partly by her sense of her lack of usefulness. The question of how middle-class women, particularly unmarried women, might spend their time was an important one in the nineteenth century. Denied entry into public life, higher education and the professions for much of the period, they frequently spent time on domestic duties and social calls. Florence Nightingale, in a piece entitled 'Cassandra' (written in 1852 but unpublished until 1928), lamented the social structures and gender ideologies that meant that middle- and upper-class women were prevented from performing fulfilling work, and argued that the idle nature of their lives was likely to cause acute mental distress, asking, 'Why have women passion, intellect, moral activity – these three – and a place in society where no one of the three can be exercised?' She thus echoes Caroline Helstone's experience in *Shirley*. Determined to overcome the feelings of melancholy and depression that are the result of her own perceived lack of useful activity and fulfilment, Caroline resolves to find work as a governess, but is dissuaded from doing so by her friends and family: as there is no financial need for her to work, they cannot comprehend why she would submit herself to the difficulties of a governess's life, failing to recognise the significance of her desire for a useful, purposeful existence.

Brontë knew from experience the hardships governesses were subject to, and the objections raised to Caroline's proposal are in many ways legitimate: the point Brontë sought to make was that women in Caroline's position desired some kind of occupation or vocation, and should be entitled to it. Yet their options were extremely limited, and it is these limitations that she attempts to explore and to highlight through Caroline's plight in *Shirley*. From a feminist perspective, however, Brontë does not offer any satisfactory solution to these problems. Indeed, the problem of how Caroline might usefully spend her time is ultimately resolved by her marriage to Robert Moore at the conclusion of the novel. The implication is thus that marriage represents an acceptable alternative to work, and that the problem of how women might usefully occupy their time is one that pertains only to single women: the married woman's time would, she seems to suggest, inevitably be spent on wifely and maternal duties, and this would necessarily assuage any desire to work. Earlier in the novel, when Caroline expresses a desire for a profession, Shirley, echoing the conservative view of the time, argues that 'hard labour and learned professions, they say, make women masculine, coarse, unwomanly,' to which Caroline responds, 'What does it signify, whether unmarried and never-to-be-married women are unattractive and inelegant, or not?' The question supports the suggestion that Brontë is only concerned with the *single* woman's right to work. While the view that marriage was sufficient occupation for women was prevalent at the time, Charlotte's friend Mary Taylor was outraged by what she saw as a retreat from the question of women's right to work. Writing to Charlotte a few months after the publication of *Shirley*, she effectively accused her of betraying her sex:

> I have seen some extracts from Shirley in which you talk of women working. And this first duty, this great necessity you seem to think that <u>some</u> women may indulge in – if they give up marriage & don't make themselves too disagreeable to the other sex. You are a coward & a traitor. A woman who works is by that alone better than one who does not.

As with so much of her fiction, Charlotte's views on women and work as expressed in *Shirley* were undoubtedly influenced by her own experiences: by the time *Shirley* was published, Charlotte was thirty-three years old; had she retained any hope of marrying, this must surely have been abandoned following the deaths of her siblings. She had long been concerned about her father's health, and her sense of obligation to him would have prevented her considering any proposal that would lead to her removal from the family home at Haworth. It is therefore not entirely surprising that Brontë concerns herself with the plight of single women in *Shirley*.

While her own status as an unmarried woman appears to have influenced her portrayal of Caroline Helstone in *Shirley*, inevitably, Charlotte's recent losses are also reflected in the novel. Having begun writing *Shirley* some months before Branwell's death, she had completed a significant proportion of the novel by the time he died. The writing process was, however, interrupted by the spate of deaths, and by the time she returned to the work she was attempting to reconcile herself to her new position as the sole survivor of Patrick and Maria's six children. She later confessed that 'the last volume [...] was composed in the eager, restless endeavour to combat mental sufferings that were scarcely tolerable.' One of the effects of her siblings' deaths while she was writing the novel was the inclusion of a number of fictional characters and episodes that are rooted in her own painful experiences. Gaskell claimed that the character of Shirley was based on Emily Brontë, 'as [she] would have been, had she been placed in health and prosperity' (critics have speculated that the original of the novel's second heroine, Caroline Helstone, was Ellen Nussey, Anne Brontë, or Charlotte herself). There is a nod towards Anne's first novel in the naming of Mrs Pryor: her maiden name is Miss Gray, and we learn subsequently that her Christian name is Agnes. Returning to *Shirley* following the death of Anne, Charlotte began the third volume of the novel with the chapter entitled 'The Valley of the Shadow of Death', in which Caroline becomes seriously ill, and hovers for some time between life and death. Unlike Charlotte's sisters, however, her heroine recovers from her illness – her recovery hastened by the revelation that Mrs Pryor is her lost mother. While reality had become almost unbearable for Charlotte by this point, her fiction provided a source of much-needed escapism: Caroline survives, as Emily and Anne had not; she is reunited with her mother, as Charlotte could never be. Indeed, there has been speculation that Charlotte originally intended that Caroline should die, but that she altered the plot of the novel in light of her sisters' deaths. Having initially struggled to complete the novel, her writing now became a source of comfort and catharsis, as her private grief infiltrated and coloured her public writing, contributing to the somewhat contradictory nature of the novel.

Shirley's disjointedness is emphasised in some of the reviews it generated, and is perhaps part of the reason it has failed to exert the same influence and fascination on generations of readers as *Jane Eyre*. There was general agreement amongst the first reviewers of *Shirley* on two points: firstly, that the novel was inferior to its predecessor; secondly, that it was the work of a woman writer. Aspects of the text were singled out for more severe criticism: the portrayal of the male characters; the reversal of the Jane/Rochester relationship through Shirley and Louis; and the opening chapter – which was particularly derided. Charlotte was somewhat disappointed with the response to *Shirley*, bemoaning the fact that it was 'disparaged in comparison with "Jane Eyre"', when she had spent 'more time, thought and anxiety' on it. She was also, inevitably, somewhat distressed by the widely held assumption that Currer Bell was the pseudonym of a woman writer. Writing to James Taylor at Smith, Elder and Co. she confessed, 'I imagined – mistakenly as it now appears – that "Shirley" bore fewer traces of the female hand than "Jane Eyre": that I have misjudged disappoints me a little – though I cannot exactly see where the error lies.' Henceforth, however, she would have to resign herself to the fact that her sex was known to readers and reviewers. While this may initially have been a source of some anguish, the resolution of this aspect of her public and private selves arguably enabled her to develop as a writer, and to produce, in her next and final novel *Villette*, her most mature work.

Final Years

Some of the difficulties Charlotte had faced in completing *Shirley* were to plague her again with *Villette*. Grief and her now relatively solitary life at Haworth contributed significantly to the writer's block with which she perpetually suffered. In her biography of the Brontës, Juliet Barker argues that Haworth was far from being the obscure, isolated Yorkshire village imagined by Brontë mythologists, noting that it was rapidly expanding in population at the time the Brontë family resided there, and that it was located within relatively easy distance of three major towns: Bradford, Halifax and Burnley. While this is undoubtedly true, in a letter to Ellen Nussey shortly after her return from Brussels, Charlotte herself described Haworth as 'a lonely, quiet spot, buried away from the world', and the popular image of Haworth stems in part from the largely self-imposed isolation of the Brontë sisters, who frequently eschewed society in favour of each other's company. This is apparent in some of Charlotte's earliest surviving letters: writing to Ellen Nussey in 1835 at the age of eighteen, she refers to her as 'almost the only, and certainly the dearest friend I possess (out of our own family)'. Patrick Brontë, recalling his children's early years at Haworth, notes, 'As they had few opportunities, of being in learned, and polished society in their retired country situation they formed a little society amongst themselves – with which they seem'd contented and happy.' This 'little society' had survived into adulthood, but while this self-imposed isolation may have been welcome whilst her siblings lived, the loneliness of her existence quickly became apparent after their deaths. Even in the immediacy of her grief after Anne's death, she recognised the change that would now inevitably take place. Discussing the future in a letter to her publisher, she writes:

> May I retain strength and cheerfulness enough to be a comfort to [Papa] and to bear up against the weight of the solitary life to come – it will be solitary – I cannot help dreading the first experience of it – the first aspect of the empty rooms which once were tenanted by those dearest to my heart – and where the shadow of their last days must now – I think – linger for ever.

A few days later, she wrote to Ellen Nussey, 'Solitude may be cheered and made endurable beyond what I can believe. The great trial is when evening closes and night approaches – At that hour we used to assemble in the dining-room – we used to talk – Now I sit by myself – necessarily I am silent.' Brontë began her career as one of three writers, collaborating initially on the collection of poems, and advising and discussing their later fiction. She now had to learn to write unaided, without the help and advice of her lost sisters. Though her solitary life became gradually more endurable, she battled grief, solitude and depression of spirits for a long time following the deaths of her sisters, and her ability to write suffered accordingly. She had hoped that grief and loneliness might be assuaged by throwing herself into her work, but the solitude left her severely depressed and she found it difficult to concentrate on her writing. She was reluctant to spend any significant time away from Haworth, despite the effect this might have on her depressed spirits, as she was increasingly aware of her duty to her father as his last surviving child. Thus, Charlotte's domestic role and her role as a writer once again appeared in conflict with one another.

While struggling to finish what would be her final completed novel, Charlotte was approached by her publishers and asked if she would consider editing a new volume of her sisters' novels, *Wuthering Heights* and *Agnes Grey*. She agreed, and this was to prove a painful but cathartic process that would ultimately assist in the overcoming of her writer's block and enable her to complete *Villette*. If *Shirley* in some ways embodies Brontë's struggle between her public self as writer and her private self as grieving sister, this is further emphasised in her treatment of her sisters' works following their deaths. Writing the Preface for this new edition, Charlotte took it upon herself to issue a partial defence of her sisters' works, which had come in for some criticism from reviewers (particularly *Wuthering Heights* and *The Tenant of Wildfell Hall*). Though her stated purpose was to 'wipe the dust off their gravestones, and leave their dear names free from soil', Charlotte was also keen to emphasise once again that Currer, Ellis and Acton Bell were three separate authors, and began the Biographical Note that was to introduce the edition by reiterating this. It was, perhaps, her desire to distinguish her own work from that of her sisters that led to her somewhat patronising and critical assessment of her sisters' work. Discussing *Wuthering Heights*, she alludes to Emily's 'immature' power of composition, echoing some of the critical reviews of that novel, and goes on to note that her sister 'had no worldly wisdom'. In the 'Editor's Preface' that followed the Biographical Note, she expands on what she perceives as the faults with Emily's novel, reserving particular criticism for the characters of Heathcliff and Catherine, patronisingly declaring, 'Having formed these beings, she did not know what she had done,' and concluding that it was scarcely advisable to create characters such as Heathcliff.

Though critical of *Wuthering Heights*, Charlotte reserved her harshest criticism for Anne's second novel, *The Tenant of Wildfell Hall*. She declared that her sister's 'choice of subject was an entire mistake' – the result, she proposed, of a tendency towards religious melancholy. Her criticism of Anne's second novel suggests again the extent to which she was influenced by reviewers: though she sought to defend her own work in the face of unfavourable reviews, her response to criticism of her sisters' work seems to have been to agree with those criticisms. However, while she clearly disapproved of Anne's focus in *The Tenant of Wildfell Hall*, a brief passage at the conclusion of *The Professor* suggests that she nevertheless might have sympathised with the plight of her sister's heroine. William Crimsworth, the eponymous professor, asks his wife, Frances, 'what she would have been had she married a harsh, envious, careless man – a profligate, a prodigal, a drunkard, or a tyrant' – a description that anticipates the character of Arthur Huntingdon in Anne's second novel. The exchange between the couple is significant in light of Charlotte's later criticism of her sister's novel, and indeed the parallels with *The Tenant of Wildfell Hall* are such that the scene may even have influenced Anne's work. Frances replies:

'I should have tried to endure the evil or cure it for awhile; and when I found it intolerable and incurable, I should have left my torturer suddenly and silently.'

'And if law or might had forced you back again?'

'What, to a drunkard, a profligate, a selfish spendthrift, and unjust fool?'

'Yes.'

'I would have gone back; again assured myself whether or not his vice and my misery were capable of remedy; and if not, have left him again.'

While Charlotte thus appears to have sympathised with the figure of the abused wife, the subject is merely a footnote in her novel, and her later criticism of Anne's work suggests she did not consider it a suitable topic for further exploration.

Charlotte's criticism of her sisters' work, so soon after their deaths when the pain of their loss was still raw, seems extraordinary. The motivation for this is suggested by the opening of her

Preface, in which she alludes to the fact that, despite numerous assertions to the contrary, there remained a popular belief that Currer, Acton and Ellis Bell were one and the same person. Given the critical response to *Wuthering Heights* and *The Tenant of Wildfell Hall*, and Charlotte's tendency to take criticism of her work to heart, it is perhaps not surprising that she sought to distance herself from her sisters' work. In a sense, the Preface marks the clashing of the public and private worlds of Charlotte Brontë, the collision of her personal and public selves. Seeking to protect her own reputation as a writer, she publicly disparages her sisters' works, despite the grief she still suffered at their loss. Her denunciation of *The Tenant of Wildfell Hall* has led to speculation that, motivated by a similar desire to avoid association with work that she considered unwise in its choice of subject, she may have destroyed Emily's second novel. There is little direct evidence to support this, although there exists a letter from Thomas Newby to Ellis Bell that alludes to her second novel, and a letter from Charlotte to her own publishers, written shortly before Emily's death, in which she seeks to dispel the rumour that Newby is to publish a further work by Ellis and Acton Bell. While, as some scholars have suggested, this may have been an error on Newby's part and his letter may in fact have been intended for Anne Brontë, it nevertheless seems strange that Emily should have ceased to write at the time when her sisters were busy working on their next novels. Further, in light of Charlotte's criticism of her sisters' works, there can be little doubt that if she discovered her sister's unpublished work following her death and deemed it unfit, for whatever reason, for public consumption, she would have suppressed it, perhaps in an attempt to protect her sister's reputation.

The new edition of *Wuthering Heights* and *Agnes Grey* was published in December 1850. Shortly after, Charlotte made a short trip to the Lake District to visit the writer Harriet Martineau, whom she had initially met on her visit to London in 1849. This was followed by a visit to Ellen Nussey at Birstall, which had the effect of significantly improving her spirits. Over the course of the year 1851, she received various visitors at the parsonage, including, in April, James Taylor, who worked for her publishers, Smith, Elder and Co. Charlotte's correspondence with Ellen Nussey suggests that Taylor may have proposed, or at the very least hinted at the possibility of marriage. Charlotte was at this time thirty-five years old, and she had long ago accepted that she would probably never marry. She refused to consider James Taylor as a potential husband, in spite of the fact that her father, who had appeared distinctly averse to the idea of a marriage, seemed to welcome the prospect (as long as it was sufficiently delayed). Charlotte, however, found him neither physically attractive nor her intellectual equal. The notion that she was better off single than married to a man she could not respect thus appears to have continued to hold sway for her.

In addition to receiving guests in Haworth, Charlotte made a number of trips, to Manchester and London among other places, the latter provoking rumours that she was to be married there, which she laughingly dismissed. During her stay in London she visited the Great Exhibition at Crystal Palace a number of times (describing it as 'a marvellous, stirring, bewildering sight'), and attended several lectures by Thackeray. The effect of this activity seems to have been to keep at bay, to some extent at least, the bouts of depression she had increasingly suffered following her siblings' deaths (particularly around the time of the anniversary of their passing), though it also contributed to the delay in completing *Villette*; indeed when alone at Haworth she continued to suffer from bouts of melancholy – writing in one letter to Ellen Nussey, 'I endure life – but whether I enjoy it or not is another question.' She continued to worry about her father's health, and in a revealing letter to Ellen Nussey written in March 1851, their mutual friend Mary Taylor refers, in what seems now a terrible irony given that she was to predecease her father, to the possible effect of Patrick's death on Charlotte's 'weakened painstruck mind'. In December of that year, however,

Emily's dog, Keeper, died, shortly before the anniversary of Emily's death, and this, along with a series of minor health complaints, was partly responsible for the return of Charlotte's feelings of melancholy and depression. Medical treatment only served to exacerbate the situation – resulting in mercury poisoning at the close of the year – all of which further delayed the completion of *Villette*.

With the exception of the mercury poisoning, the minor complaints that Charlotte suffered at this time were ailments to which she was prone throughout her adult life. Her letters are punctuated with references to her apparently persistent ill health – to coughs, colds, nervous headaches, stomach problems and so forth – which has led to accusations of hypochondria being levelled at the author by biographers and scholars. While there may be some truth in this, the prolonged bouts of melancholy to which she was prone, along with symptoms such as sleeplessness and loss of appetite, which tended to manifest themselves particularly during times of solitude at Haworth, suggest she suffered from clinical depression, one of the symptoms of which was her tendency towards hypochondria. Such a tendency is hardly surprising given her earlier bereavements. Her concerns over tuberculosis, the disease that had claimed the lives of all five of her siblings, led her to speculate about her own condition whenever she suffered from bouts of ill health, and to worry that she too might succumb to the disease. Charlotte's depression was exacerbated by her solitude: though she lived with her father and servants, she spent extended periods alone. Her father kept largely to his study, and the household kept early hours; consequently Charlotte frequently spent her evenings, when the light and her poor eyesight prevented her from reading, in quiet reflection, often dwelling on the past and contrasting her position with the time when her sisters were still alive: 'memory', she wrote to her publisher, 'is both sad and relentless'.

Evidence that Charlotte suffered from depression is to be found throughout her letters: as well as the frequent references to a depressed spirit and periods of melancholy, she refers to being 'tormented' by 'erratic and vague instincts' and declares 'my life is a pale blank and often a very weary burden,' 'I feel fettered – incapable.' It is clear that her grief at her sisters' deaths remained raw, and any reminder of their passing plunged her further into despair. Receiving a letter from Mary Taylor, now resident in New Zealand, informing her of a cousin's death, she wrote to Ellen, 'It ripped up half-scarred wounds with terrible force – the death-bed was just the same – breath failing &c.' Charlotte continued to battle with periods of severe depression for several years after her sisters' deaths – only eventually finding relief, somewhat surprisingly given her earlier attitude, through her marriage.

Charlotte's letters from 1851 contain almost no mention of the novel that she had begun in early 1850, and the difficulties in completing *Villette* continued well into the following year: writing to Margaret Wooler in March 1852, she informed her that it had been nearly four months since she had worked on the novel. In this respect, her sisters' deaths had a profound effect not only on her personal life, but on her public life as a writer as well: a crucial effect of their deaths was the removal of the literary advice and support she had received as she strove to write *Jane Eyre* and a significant portion of *Shirley*. Her writer's block was partly rooted in a sense of her reliance on her own judgment now that Emily and Anne were no longer there. Frustrated and disappointed by her failure to complete *Villette*, she resolved to refuse all invitations until after it was completed. This did not, however, prevent her from making a pilgrimage to Filey in East Yorkshire in the summer. She stayed in the guest house where she and Ellen had stayed following Anne Brontë's death three years previously, and visited her sister's grave at Scarborough, discovering a number of errors on the gravestone and ordering that they be rectified. Shortly after she returned to Haworth, her father fell seriously ill, and for a short time his life seemed threatened, further adding to Charlotte's anxieties. Eventually, in October 1852, she sent the first two volumes of *Villette* to her publishers, and worked determinedly to finish the third, finally completing and submitting it towards the end of November.

Now an established writer, whose identity was generally known, she remained anxious that her work be judged on its literary merits alone, and asked her publisher to consider anonymous publication – with no reference to Currer Bell, Charlotte Brontë or her previous works. This request was an attempt to ensure that *Villette* was not judged on the basis of or alongside her previous novels, but in its own right – undoubtedly partly influenced by the unfavourable comparisons reviewers had made between *Shirley* and *Jane Eyre*. However, Smith, Elder and Co. were, understandably, reluctant to agree to this request: the author of *Jane Eyre* was, after all, extremely marketable, whereas an anonymous novel would struggle to receive notice in the periodicals of the day. Charlotte was thus persuaded to abandon this idea, and the novel was published in January 1853, once again under the pseudonym of 'Currer Bell', despite the fact that her true identity was now widely known. Further, the title page reminded the reader that 'Currer Bell' was the 'Author of "Jane Eyre", "Shirley", etc.', so Charlotte was unable to avoid comparisons with her earlier works.

Villette, as many of her contemporaries agreed, is Charlotte Brontë's most mature work. While she was relatively unsuccessful in negotiating the criticisms of *Jane Eyre* whilst constructing *Shirley*, the critical reviews of her second novel seem to have been used to better effect in improving her writing. *Villette* shifts from the historical setting of *Shirley* to a contemporary setting, whilst also shifting from the familiar landscape of Yorkshire to a less familiar European setting (in this respect, as well as in some of the plot details, *Villette* is a partial reworking of Charlotte's first novel, *The Professor*, which remained unpublished). Perhaps in response to criticisms of her treatment of class and the woman question in *Shirley*, Charlotte sought to avoid offering any kind of social commentary in *Villette*, a fact made clear in a letter to her publishers, in which she declares, 'I cannot write books handling the topics of the day – it is of no use trying.' The focus of her final novel, then, is on the experiences of the heroine, although Lucy Snowe is perhaps the least likeable of all Brontë's heroines: as her name suggests (and as Charlotte intended), she is a somewhat cold character, and frustrates the reader by withholding significant information from her narrative (the fact that Dr John and Graham Bretton are one and the same person, for instance). Though Dr John is more typical of the nineteenth-century hero, Brontë dismisses the possibility of the heroine's union with him, and instead sets the scene for her marriage to Paul Emanuel – a character based on M. Heger, suggesting that she was still battling her feelings for him, despite having left Brussels almost a decade earlier.

However, perhaps influenced by her own single status, Charlotte refused to provide the typical happy-ever-after ending for her heroine. Instead, the novel concludes on a note of uncertainty which suggests the possibility that Paul Emanuel has been lost at sea, but leaves open the possibility of his rescue and subsequent marriage to the heroine. The ambiguous conclusion to *Villette* is in stark contrast to the typical Victorian novel, with its emphasis on 'neat' endings – usually through death or marriage. In offering both possibilities, *Villette* seems to anticipate modernist fiction, which emerged over half a century later and frequently defined itself in contradistinction to Victorian narrative forms. In reality, the conclusion to *Villette*, though representing in some respects an experiment in fiction, was partly the result of Patrick Brontë's influence: her father had an aversion to works that concluded on a depressing note, and was keen that Charlotte provide a happy ending to her novel. Having already conceived the notion of Paul Emanuel's death, Charlotte only partly conceded to her father's wishes, by leaving open the possibility of the heroine's marriage for those readers inclined to picture it. This ambiguity resulted in readers of the novel writing to the author to demand to know her hero's fate, but she refused to provide any concrete answers. Writing to her publisher regarding the ending, her own preference is clear:

> Drowning and Matrimony are the fearful alternatives. The merciful [...] will of course choose the former and milder doom – drown him to put him out of pain. The cruel-hearted will on the contrary pitilessly impale him on the second horn of the dilemma – marrying him without ruth or compunction.

This letter, written in March 1853, makes it clear that Charlotte remained resigned to – even welcomed – her single status, and had no intention of marrying. It is somewhat surprising, then, that the following year, she would herself choose the path she appears to reject for her heroine, and marry her father's curate, Arthur Bell Nicholls.

Shortly before the publication of *Villette*, with the novel completed and her literary career back on track, Charlotte's personal life took an unexpected turn. With her reputation as a writer assured, and having refused several earlier proposals of marriage, at the age of thirty-six it seemed as though Charlotte had chosen the professional life of a writer over the domestic life of a wife and mother. However, at the close of 1852, she received another proposal of marriage – from Arthur Bell Nicholls, whom by this time she had known for several years. Like her earlier would-be suitors, Nicholls was refused – hardly surprising given her earlier assessment of him as a 'highly uninteresting, narrow and unattractive specimen of the "coarser sex"'. Two years later, however, she was to reconsider her decision and to marry Nicholls. Though Charlotte professed to be content with her single status, she was undoubtedly pained by the loneliness of her existence, and her father's continuing ill health must inevitably have rendered the future particularly bleak. 'I am a lonely woman and likely to be lonely,' she wrote to Ellen around this time: 'this excessive solitude presses too heavily.' Nevertheless, her initial inclination was to reject Nicholls' proposal, which appears to have been largely unexpected, despite several years' acquaintance. Patrick Brontë reacted angrily to what he perceived as his curate's presumption in proposing to his daughter. Indeed, though Charlotte informed Ellen that she did not love Nicholls, her rejection of him was at least partly influenced by her father's reaction, which was such on her informing him of the proposal that she hastily agreed to refuse Nicholls. Though initially disinclined to marry him, she was nevertheless distressed by her father's behaviour, which, along with Charlotte's refusal, led Nicholls to make arrangements to leave Haworth, where he had resided for the last eight years. He left in May 1853, deeply distressed at the prospect of moving away from the woman he loved. Though Charlotte sympathised deeply with him, she could not offer him the consolation he sought, and resigned herself to the probability, with some relief admittedly, that she would never see him again.

Life in Haworth continued much as before, with Charlotte suffering intermittent bouts of ill health, making various trips, and receiving the occasional visitor. In September 1853, Elizabeth Gaskell visited Haworth for the first time, and the impression the visit made on her was to have a great effect on her later portrayal of Charlotte and her home in *The Life of Charlotte Brontë*, first published four years later. She witnessed directly the solitary nature of Charlotte's daily life, the beauty and desolation of the surrounding moors, and what she perceived as the eccentricity of Patrick Brontë's character. Charlotte discussed Nicholls' proposal and her father's reaction to it with her friend, and on returning to Manchester, Gaskell, convinced that Patrick Brontë's antipathy to Nicholls was rooted primarily in the latter's lack of money, surreptitiously began to make enquiries about a possible pension for Charlotte's would-be suitor, in the hope that her friend would reconsider his proposal.

Gaskell's belief that Nicholls' suit was not entirely hopeless proved correct. Nicholls returned to Haworth on a visit in July 1853, and on his departure Charlotte entered into regular correspondence with him. Though Gaskell was keen to further Charlotte's relationship with Nicholls, Ellen Nussey strongly disapproved, leading to a breakdown in relations between Charlotte and one of her oldest friends. It seems likely that Ellen felt threatened by Charlotte's developing relationship with Nicholls: like Charlotte, she was unmarried, and seemed to consider her friend almost under an obligation to remain thus. In a letter to their mutual friend, Mary Taylor, she suggested that marriage would render Charlotte inconsistent with herself. As a single woman, and Charlotte's closest friend outside of her immediate family for over twenty years, it is perhaps understandable that she did not welcome this new development in Charlotte's life. It appears that she said as much to Charlotte, creating a tension in their friendship that lasted several months. However, while Charlotte's relationship with Ellen entered a rocky period, her relationship with Nicholls was making significant progress. Following a further visit to Haworth, Patrick Brontë was persuaded to reconsider his disapproval of Nicholls, and by April 1854, Charlotte had accepted Nicholls's proposal, and found herself, at the age of thirty-seven, engaged to be married.

Though Ellen's attitude towards Charlotte's developing relationship with Nicholls was certainly unreasonable, her assertion that it would be inconsistent for Charlotte to marry is nevertheless borne out by Charlotte's earlier declarations on the subject of marriage, and her decision to marry at this stage in her life perhaps warrants some further explanation. It is possible, of course, that her earlier refusals were simply a matter of failing to find a man whom she wished to marry – particularly in light of her feelings for M. Heger. Nevertheless, some of her earlier letters, as well as aspects of her fiction, clearly suggest an antipathy towards marriage itself. Writing to Ellen Nussey of the forthcoming marriages of Anne's former pupils, the Misses

Robinson, several years earlier, she declares, 'They are not married yet – but expect to be married (or rather sacrificed) in the course of a few months.' Though the comment is made largely in jest, the notion of marriage as sacrifice became a common refrain in nineteenth-century feminist debates, and Charlotte's throwaway comment hints at an awareness of this. In *The Professor*, published posthumously in 1857, Frances Crimsworth hints at the potential dangers of marriage, for women in particular: 'If a wife's nature loathes that of the man she is wedded to, marriage must be slavery.'

Charlotte's decision to marry Arthur Bell Nicholls was almost certainly influenced by her continued sense of loneliness and isolation: indeed, the rift in her friendship with Ellen may, somewhat paradoxically given Ellen's attitude, have served to persuade Charlotte that marriage offered the possibility of fulfilment that had until now eluded her, in the form of constant companionship. Though she had more than fulfilled her long-held dreams of literary success, she remained, in many respects, unhappy, as the bouts of depression she suffered attest. Her earlier decision to remain single was perhaps in part a reluctance to sacrifice her independence, and particularly her literary career, in order to take up the duties of wife and mother – for motherhood would inevitably be expected to follow marriage. With her success as an author assured, she now took steps towards personal happiness and fulfilment.

Charlotte married Nicholls on 29th June 1854 in Haworth church in the presence of a small number of guests, including Miss Wooler and Ellen Nussey, with whom Charlotte was now reconciled. Patrick Brontë, pleading ill health, did not attend the ceremony, though whether this is indicative of a continued resistance to the marriage is unclear (certainly his relations with Nicholls had improved, and indeed they remained close following Charlotte's death, until Patrick's own death in 1861). It was thus left to Miss Wooler to give the bride away. The newly-weds honeymooned in Wales and Ireland, where Charlotte was introduced to her husband's family. In spite of her earlier apparent indifference, even antipathy, towards Nicholls, she appears to have found happiness through her marriage: 'My life is changed indeed,' she wrote to Ellen on her return to Haworth. In particular, her marriage seems to have proved an effective cure for her bouts of depression, as she found herself constantly in her husband's company, and thus with less opportunity to dwell on the past. Since the success of *Jane Eyre*, Charlotte had struggled to negotiate between her public and private selves, and with her marriage to Nicholls, her literary career appears to have assumed less importance in her eyes: 'If true domestic happiness replace Fame – the exchange will indeed be for the better.' It seemed, in the first few months of her marriage, that despite the tragedies that had befallen her, Charlotte Brontë had finally found personal fulfilment, and that she might consider herself fortunate in both her professional and her personal lives.

Though Charlotte seems to have been willing to relinquish her literary success in favour of a happy marriage, she continued to write, producing the first two chapters of a novel provisionally entitled *Emma*. She did not live to complete the work, but following her death the manuscript was edited and published by her husband. As with her previous works, the title suggests a focus on the experiences of the heroine, though the fragment does not introduce the reader to the eponymous Emma. Following in the tradition of *Jane Eyre*, *Shirley* and *Villette*, the opening of the novel suggests that the narrative has a partly autobiographical basis: the reader is introduced to the narrator, Mrs Chalfont, a woman 'not young nor yet old', whose life has recently been enriched by 'an interest and a companion', echoing perhaps Charlotte's recent marriage to Nicholls. The fragment describes a small school, run by sisters by the name of Wilcox, struggling to attract enough pupils to make it financially viable, and in this respect is reminiscent of the Brontë sisters' plan to open a school. The presence of a girl at the school, apparently impersonating an heiress, suggests a return to the sensationalism that characterised

Jane Eyre. There are no surviving documents detailing Charlotte's plans for the novel, but the fragment is nevertheless significant – as evidence of the author's attempts to combine her domestic and professional duties, if nothing else.

Charlotte's marriage to Nicholls, though brief, appears to have been a happy one, perhaps in part because he was willing for her to continue her literary career. Ellen, however, although now reconciled with Charlotte, remained suspicious of the union, and her fears relating to Charlotte's marriage must have appeared to have been at least partially realised when she received a letter from her friend informing her that Nicholls required from Ellen a promise that she would burn Charlotte's letters once she had read them. Ellen's ambivalent response to this request prompted Charlotte's husband to threaten to censor his wife's letters if the promise was not given. Though Charlotte treated the matter as something of a joke, Ellen was understandably infuriated by this: though she complied with the request and gave her promise, it was undoubtedly done to avoid the threatened censure, and it is unlikely that she ever intended to keep her word. Certainly, the majority of letters Charlotte wrote to Ellen appear to have survived, providing valuable insights into her character. Despite this incident, Nicholls does not appear to have been a tyrannical husband, and Charlotte's letters from this period make it clear that she was very happy in her marriage. She describes Nicholls as a 'good, kind, attached husband', declaring, 'No kinder, better husband than mine, it seems to me.' The subsidence of the symptoms of ill health that had dogged her since the death of her sisters and were undoubtedly a symptom of her depression provides further evidence of a happy marriage.

Tragically, however, Charlotte's happiness would not last long. Her marriage, though it provided an effective cure for her depressed spirits, was ultimately to lead to her premature death. In January 1855, Charlotte began to experience faintness and nausea, and suspected that she may be pregnant. The sickness persisted, becoming unrelenting: she was prevented from obtaining adequate nourishment, and began to vomit blood. By the end of January, she was confined to bed. Her condition continued to deteriorate, and at the end of March, Patrick Brontë wrote to Ellen to inform her that his daughter was on the brink of death. She died the following day, at the age of thirty-eight, along with her unborn child. Patrick's letter to Elizabeth Gaskell, written a few months after the death of his last surviving child, hints at the tragedy of her death, coming so soon after she had finally found happiness: 'The marriage that took place, seem'd to hold forth, long, and bright prospects of happiness, but in the inscrutable providence of God, all our hopes have ended in disappointment, and our joy in mourning.' Patrick was left as the sole survivor of his wife and six children. Charlotte was buried in the family vault in the church next to which she had lived almost her entire life, alongside her mother Maria, her sisters Maria, Elizabeth and Emily, and her brother Branwell. Patrick Brontë survived the last of his children by a further six years, eventually joining his family in the vault beneath the church he had served for over forty years in June 1861. Arthur Bell Nicholls survived his wife by more than fifty years. He left Haworth following the death of Patrick Brontë, and died in Ireland in 1906, having married for a second time, but leaving no children.

Upon the death of his wife, Arthur Bell Nicholls sent out black-edged funeral cards, which simply read 'In Memory of Charlotte Nicholls, who died March XXXI, MDCCCLV, Aged 38 Years.' In letters written after her marriage to Nicholls, Charlotte signs herself 'Charlotte Brontë Nicholls', suggesting that she was unwilling to relinquish the name she had sought to conceal from the public for so long. In death, however, the anonymity she had previously so ardently desired was returned with her husband's decision to obscure his wife's literary fame on the funeral card. Similarly, the original memorial stone that was placed in Haworth church, next to that recording the deaths of her mother and siblings, read, 'Adjoining lie the remains of Charlotte, wife of the Rev. Arthur Bell Nicholls, A.B., and daughter of the Rev. P.

Brontë.' She is identified here only as 'Charlotte', her roles listed as wife and daughter respectively, her identity as writer omitted. In death, then, as in life, her identity is confused: the mask she wore as a child to answer her father's questions was replaced by the mask of Currer Bell; her 'true' identity as Charlotte Brontë was again obscured through her marriage to Nicholls and the change of name this necessitated. Ultimately, however, it was the name of Charlotte Brontë that was to live on for generations to come.

Afterlife

Despite increasing popularity during her own lifetime, Brontë can hardly have foreseen the legacy she would leave behind in terms of the public fascination with her life and work. As well as the continued interest in her writing, there remains an on-going fascination with the life of the author, indicated by the perennial popularity of Brontë biographies, as well as by the flourishing Brontë tourist industry in Haworth. The Brontë home – the parsonage in the West Yorkshire village of Haworth – was converted into a museum in 1928, when it was purchased by Sir James Roberts and donated to the Brontë Society, and attracts thousands of visitors every year, anxious to witness for themselves the place where some of the most famous works in English literature were written, and where the Brontë family lived and died. The Brontë parsonage museum not only allows the interested tourist in to the place where the Brontë sisters composed all seven of their novels, along with their poetry and juvenilia, but also includes items such as the sofa on which Emily died, items of clothing worn by the sisters, and locks of Charlotte's hair. The nearby moors are largely untouched by the modern world, and remain much as they would have been during the lifetimes of the Brontës. Visitors to Haworth can call at The Black Bull, the public house frequented by Branwell Brontë, and follow the 'Brontë walk', passing by 'Brontë falls' and over the 'Brontë bridge'; Emily Brontë is alleged to have stopped to rest on the chair-shaped rock by the falls, and a few miles across the moors from Haworth stands the ruined farmhouse Top Withens, rumoured to have been the inspiration for *Wuthering Heights*, though there is no direct evidence to support this. There is a plaque in the church where Patrick Brontë preached for forty years to mark the Brontë family vault where all the family, with the exception of Anne, were interred (though much of the church was rebuilt in 1879). In the graveyard that stands between the church and the parsonage are the graves of many of the Brontës' friends and acquaintances. There is a sense, then, in which the world of the Brontës is almost tangible to the modern visitor to Haworth, perhaps accounting for some of the intense and continuing interest in the lives of Charlotte Brontë and her family.

The relationship between the siblings has also proved a matter of much speculation – from the literary collaborations of the Brontë children, to Charlotte's criticism of her sisters' work following their premature deaths. The extent of this fascination is suggested by some of the conspiracy theories surrounding the lives of the Brontës. There has been speculation about Charlotte's sexuality, for example, in light of her relationship with Ellen Nussey (though neither her letters nor her experience of marriage lend any credence to this theory), and in June 1999, the *Daily Express* newspaper carried on its front page a picture of Charlotte Brontë, with the headline 'Did Charlotte Brontë Murder Her Siblings?' In the same year, James Tully published a novel entitled *The Crimes of Charlotte Brontë*, in which Charlotte is directly implicated in her sisters' deaths. Though fictional, it was originally intended as a factual work, but the publishers refused to publish it as such (in fact, the headline in the *Express* related to Tully's novel). While such conspiracy theories may be dismissed as entirely lacking in foundation, they are nevertheless indicative of Brontë's fame: her inclusion on the front page of a tabloid newspaper some one hundred and fifty years after her death speaks volumes about the extent to which she and her work have infiltrated the popular imagination.

The ongoing fascination with the life of the Brontës is further reflected in the large number of biographies focusing on their lives and work. The earliest biography of Brontë, Elizabeth Gaskell's *The Life of Charlotte Brontë*, was written at the request of her father, Patrick Brontë, shortly after the death of his last surviving child, and was published in 1857. It has proved hugely influential, though the picture Gaskell paints of the author of *Jane Eyre* is somewhat problematic: Gaskell's relationship with the author and the survival of many of those who knew her (including her father and husband) at the time the biography was written necessarily means that there are significant absences in the text (Brontë's feelings for M. Heger, for example, are largely obscured, while a number of letters written by Brontë did not come to light until much later). Nevertheless, Gaskell's account of Brontë's life can be seen as largely responsible for creating the tragic-romantic image of the author and her siblings that prevails today. In a much later account, *The Brontë Myth*, Lucasta Miller observes that 'with the publication of Elizabeth Gaskell's *The Life of Charlotte Brontë*, she became a legend,'[9] noting that Brontë, in Gaskell's biography, is portrayed as a 'saintly heroine'.[10] Elsewhere, Elisabeth Jay argues that Gaskell 'may be said to have created, almost single-handedly, the myth of the Brontës.'[11] There is a certain irony in the notion that Gaskell's account serves to obscure the 'real' Charlotte Brontë, creating instead a kind of mythical, idealised version of the author, given the fact that Patrick Brontë desired Gaskell to produce an authorised account of his daughter's life in order to address some of the rumours and speculation in wide circulation following her death. Numerous other biographies of the Brontës have appeared since the publication of Gaskell's, creating a tradition that has served both further to elucidate, and to obscure their lives through the creation of a romanticised, often speculative, image of the family. In 1994, Juliet Barker published her extensive and detailed account in *The Brontës*, and this remains the seminal biography of the family.

Turning to Brontë's writing, while her entire oeuvre is the subject of intense scholarly and critical debate, particularly since the 1960s and the explosion of second-wave feminist literary theory, it is her most successful novel, *Jane Eyre*, that retains the strongest hold on the public imagination. Since its publication in 1847, *Jane Eyre* has been repeatedly referenced – implicitly and explicitly – in other works: plays, films, novels and art. The process of reworking and retelling Brontë's story of the poor, plain governess began shortly after the novel's publication, and the Victorian period saw a plethora of works that allude to, engage with, adapt or draw on *Jane Eyre* – including an array of dramatic productions (eight of which were collected by Patsy Stoneman in *Jane Eyre on Stage, 1848–1898*, published in 2007), and a number of sensation novels (which draw on the more sensational elements of Brontë's plot), along with feminist works such as Charlotte Perkins Gilman's short story 'The Yellow Wallpaper', which calls into question Brontë's own pseudo-feminist position by focusing on the figure of the 'mad' wife and offering a sympathetic portrayal of her descent into madness – a state partially induced by her treatment at the hands of her husband.

The process of adapting and transforming *Jane Eyre* continued in the twentieth and twenty-first centuries, with more than twenty film and television adaptations of the novel, numerous theatre productions (including *Jane Eyre: The Musical*, which premiered on Broadway in 2000) and an abundance of novels: in her 1995 Bibliography of works influenced by *Jane Eyre*, Patsy Stoneman lists some forty novels, and several more have appeared since. Some of these draw explicitly on the original text (Jean Rhys's *Wide Sargasso Sea* and Jasper Fforde's *The Eyre Affair*, for instance), while others engage more subtly with Brontë's novel – Daphne Du Maurier's *Rebecca*, Diane Setterfield's *The Thirteenth Tale*, and even J.K. Rowling's *Harry Potter* series, in which, as in *Jane Eyre*, the orphan-protagonist is forced to endure a miserable existence with uncaring relatives, before beginning a journey of self-discovery.

While echoes of *Jane Eyre* pervade contemporary literature and culture, the novel has been subject to varying interpretations by adaptors and scholars. Screen adaptations in particular tend to emphasise the romantic aspects of the story. The character of the heroine is frequently transformed from 'plain' Jane into the stereotypical beautiful heroine, and Rochester into a brooding, romantic hero: the 1996 film version, directed by Franco Zeffirelli, used the tagline 'This year's most romantic love story'. Scholarly criticism, however, has increasingly highlighted the more problematic aspects of Brontë's narrative – in particular the author's representation of the mad wife, and Jane's equally problematic (from a feminist perspective) union with Rochester at the conclusion of the narrative.

Charlotte Brontë's life and works have resulted in a legacy that it is difficult to overestimate and which shows no signs of abating. The wealth of material inspired by *Jane Eyre* alone forms a direct retort to Southey's assertion that 'Literature cannot be the business of a woman's life: and it ought not to be.' Literature was to become the business of Brontë's life, and her life and works in turn have become profitable businesses themselves.

Notes

1. Elisabeth Jay, Introduction to Elizabeth Gaskell, *The Life of Charlotte Brontë* (London: Penguin, 2004), p. xxvi.
2. Cited in Juliet Barker, *The Brontës* (London: Phoenix, 1995), p. 42.
3. See Juliet Barker, *The Brontës*, p. 78 for further discussion.
4. Winifred Gérin, in her biography of Anne Brontë, suggests that Miss Branwell 'ruled by a tyranny of spirit, exercising her dominion by a strong appeal to the emotions over which, in the case of children with such heightened imaginations, she had an easy victory' and argues that she was partly responsible for the religious crisis Anne Brontë experienced later in life (Winifred Gérin, *Anne Brontë: A Biography* [London: Allen Lane, 1976], p. 35).
5. Advertisement for School for Clergymen's Daughters, *Leeds Intelligencer*, December 1844 in Juliet Barker, *The Brontës: A Life in Letters* (London: Viking, 1997) p. 5.
6. 'Admissions Register of the Clergy Daughters' School, Cowan Bridge' in Barker, *The Brontës: A Life in Letters*, p. 7.
7. Mark 10:9; Matthew 19:6. Prior to the 1857 Matrimonial Causes Act, divorce was only possible through an Act of Parliament. The Act made it easier for couples to divorce legally, but opponents frequently cited the Bible as evidence that, from a religious perspective at least, divorce – the separation of those joined in holy union – was effectively impossible.
8. In Barker, *The Brontës: A Life in Letters*, p. 165.
9. Lucasta Miller, *The Brontë Myth* (London: Vintage, 2001) p. 1.
10. Ibid, p. 2.
11. Jay, Introduction to *The Life of Charlotte Brontë*, p. ix.

Select bibliography

A bibliography of Brontë biography and criticism would more than fill a volume of this size, so the list below is necessarily selective. There are numerous different editions of Charlotte Brontë's novels, though critical editions such as Oxford, Penguin, Norton and Broadview are generally the most informative. There are dozens of biographies of Charlotte Brontë and her family; I include some of the most influential. The field of Brontë criticism continues to flourish: again, I have listed only a few of what I consider to be the seminal works in this field.

Allott, Miriam, ed., *The Brontës: The Critical Heritage* (London, 1974)

Barker, Juliet, *The Brontës* (London, 1994); *The Brontës: A Life in Letters* (London, 1997)

Brontë Studies: Journal of the Brontë Society (Leeds)

Eagleton, Terry, *Myths of Power: A Marxist Study of the Brontës* (London, 1975)

Fraser, Rebecca, *Charlotte Brontë* (London, 1988)

Gaskell, Elizabeth, *The Life of Charlotte Brontë* (London, 1857)

Gérin, Winifred, *Charlotte Brontë: The Evolution of Genius* (Oxford, 1967)

Gilbert, Sandra M, and Susan Gubar, *The Madwoman in the Attic: The Woman Writer and the Nineteenth-Century Literary Imagination* (New Haven, 1979)

Glen, Heather, ed., *The Cambridge Companion to the Brontës* (Cambridge, 2002); *Jane Eyre* (Basingstoke, 1997)

Gordon, Lyndall, *Charlotte Brontë: A Passionate Life* (London, 1995)

Homans, Margaret, *Bearing the Word: Language and Female Experience in Nineteenth-Century Women's Writing* (Chicago, 1986)

Ingham, Patricia, *The Brontës* (Oxford, 2006)

Kaplan, Cora, *Victoriana: Histories, Fictions, Criticisms,* (Edinburgh, 2007)

Miller, Lucasta, *The Brontë Myth* (London, 2001)

Poovey, Mary, *Uneven Developments: The Ideological Work of Gender in Mid-Victorian England* (London, 1988)

Rubik, Margarete, and Elke Mettinger-Schartmann, ed., *A Breath of Fresh Eyre: Intertextual and Intermedial Reworkings of* Jane Eyre (Amsterdam, 2007)

Showalter, Elaine, *A Literature of Their Own: From Charlotte Brontë to Doris Lessing* (London, 1978); *The Female Malady: Women, Madness and English Culture, 1830–1980* (London, 1987)

Smith, Margaret, *The Letters of Charlotte Brontë* (Oxford, 1995)

Stoneman, Patsy, *Brontë Transformations: The Cultural Dissemination of* Jane Eyre *and* Wuthering Heights (Hemel Hempstead, 1996); ed., *Jane Eyre on Stage, 1848–1898* (Aldershot, 2007)

Williams, Judith, *Perception and Expression in the Novels of Charlotte Brontë* (Ann Arbor, 1988)

Acknowledgments

Quotations from letters are taken from Margaret Smith (ed.), *The Letters of Charlotte Brontë* (Oxford: Clarendon, 1995), unless otherwise stated. Quotations from the works of Charlotte Brontë and from Elizabeth Gaskell's *The Life of Charlotte Brontë* are from the Penguin Classics editions unless otherwise stated. Quotations from reviews of the Brontës' works are taken from Miriam Allott (ed.), *The Brontës: The Critical Heritage* (London: Routledge and Kegan Paul, 1974).

Biographical note

Jessica Cox is a lecturer in English Literature at Brunel University. She has published a number of articles on Victorian literature, including the work of the Brontës, and is the editor of the Penguin edition of Charlotte Brontë's *Shirley*.